# NILGIRI
## Mountain Railway (NMR)
### FROM LIFELINE TO OBLIVION

C000192705

V.M. GOVIND KRISHNAN

INDIA · SINGAPORE · MALAYSIA

# Notion Press

Old No. 38, New No. 6
McNichols Road, Chetpet
Chennai - 600 031

First Published by Notion Press 2018
Copyright © V.M. Govind Krishnan 2018
All Rights Reserved.

ISBN 978-1-64249-487-7

# Dedication

This book is dedicated to the memory of my late grandmother, Mrs. Subhadra Chettur, whose interest in this hill railway, since my childhood, culminated in several journeys up and down the Nilgiri Hills, solely by train.

She had strongly supported my interest on this mountain railway as I watched the trains chugging and whistling in the valley below my home, while perched on a branch of a plum tree!

# Contents

# Acknowledgements

This book has been put together largely due to my own interest in the survival of the unique Nilgiri Mountain Railway (NMR), for which I had to seek the assistance of several of my friends and relatives; to send me newspaper cuttings, and any other material on this scenic railway that they chanced upon. I thank all of them wholeheartedly for their cooperation in my efforts, since 1968 - to thwart the proposed dismantling of the line; and create public awareness. Undoubtedly, this has helped this engineering marvel in being conferred the UNESCO World Heritage Site status in July 2005.

I thank my late mother, Mrs. V.M. Padmini, for collecting information pertaining to the NMR and for overseeing the Black Beauty contest at Coonoor. The idea of writing the book was largely due to her exhortation.

I also thank my sister-in-law Premila, who had meticulously collected news-clips, despite her tight work schedule; and my wife Usha for her encouragement.

I express my gratitude to Dr. G.V.J.A. Harshavardhan of Vaccine Institute, the former Station Masters at Coonoor, namely V. Nandakumar, Radhakrishnan, and T. Raveendranathan, and also the foreman of the Loco Shed at Coonoor for their cooperation and valuable inputs.

My good friend, P.S. Sundar, a noted journalist and orator, was of immense help being a strong supporter of the NMR and who actively participated to bring publicity to this marvel of engineering skill. He prodded the Railway authorities to run the existing train service, as otherwise this magnificent marvel of engineering would have drifted into oblivion.

Special thanks are due to my son, Arvind, for his unstinted assistance to "computerise" the entire text, to scan the photographs and colour slides, and to have any amendments effected. Several videos of this railway, taken by both of us, can be viewed worldwide at this site: **http://www.youtube.com/user/arvindkrishnan**

If by oversight I have left somebody out of this list, my sincere apologies and thank you all the same.

I assume responsibility for any kind of errors which may have inadvertently crept into the compilation, for which I may please be excused.

# Prologue

A marvel of engineering skill - the Nilgiri Mountain Railway (NMR), has been in the news for a long time, ever since the Ministry of Railways in India proposed to dismantle the scenic railway in 1968 owing to "uneconomic working". It was then included in the list of branch lines to be closed. Official indifference played havoc with this unique mountain railway, and, being far away from the seat of the government no effort was made to improve services on the line. Time and again proposals to dismantle the line have come up, but public protest has kept it going. However, after this railway was given the status of a World Heritage site by UNESCO in July 2005, the Indian Railway authorities began to take note of their asset.

This book is a tribute to the relentless campaign by railway enthusiasts and the public of the Nilgiri Hills to keep the beautiful engineering marvel in running condition. Their untiring effort continues to this day, and it is largely due to this that the unique railway has got recognition as a World Heritage site by UNESCO on July 15, 2005.

The information given in this book comprises a vast collection of letters, articles, and news clips from various newspapers and magazines spread over a period of fifty years; which makes the Nilgiri Mountain Railway the most written about railway in the world.

The credit goes to all those who have assisted me in obtaining the newspaper cuttings, and to those who sincerely contributed to the survival of the now hundred and eighteen years old mountain railway – the only one of its kind in Asia, built in the erstwhile British regime in India.

Though some may dub me a 'madcap' for having collected so much information and newspaper cuttings on the Nilgiri Mountain Railway, I do believe Shakespeare's words that *"there's method in this madness."* How else would I be able to compile so much information in a book on the past five decades of the struggle for survival of this magnificent railway? This book could serve as an almanac on the NMR as all events are chronologically arranged to depict the true picture, as also the public opinion which helped thwart the moves of the government of India to close the line.

Among the 'steam enthusiasts' who, in recent times, have made known the existence of this railway are travel columnist Bill Aitken, Sir Mark Tully - former BBC (India) Chief of Bureau, and R.R. Bhandari - a top official with Indian Railways who has authored several books on India's railways including those owned by the former Princely States.

My own interest in the NMR originated in my childhood days, when I used to watch the trains from my hilltop abode, "Vita Nuova," at Mount Pleasant, Coonoor. The view of the valley and hills around was stunning, as also the view of the railway track and the far away railway bridge at Wellington. On my way to school situated on a hill opposite to where I stayed, I had to trek down the valley and cross a railway bridge spanning a brook below and watch the train to Ooty chugging uphill in a fury of steam amidst a clatter of piston rods; and belching clouds of grayish-black smoke. This was truly a poetry in motion and it remains forever etched in my mind.

The punctuality of the trains in those days was highly commendable and one could set the watch according to the train passing by. Sadly, this is not the case nowadays as the solitary Nilagiri Passenger (formerly Nilagiri Express, more romantically known as Blue Mountain Express) from Mettupalayam to Ooty almost invariably runs behind time by up to two hours, as the vintage Swiss steam engines have lost much of their pushing power necessitating in more time at the intermediate halts en route for panting and reflection. Also, at times the train gets stranded en route as the coal supply in the loco is fully exhausted even before the train could reach Coonoor, ostensibly due to poor quality of coal stocked by the Southern Railway. Such things were unheard of in the past. This happened even after conversion of old engines to run on furnace oil instead of coal.

During my career in Air-India spanning almost 34 years, I have made "steam enthusiasts" of many of my colleagues, some of whom travelled by the NMR on their honeymoon. I also had the opportunity to interact with other steam enthusiasts, notably Ashwani Lohani, the then Director, National Rail Museum, New Delhi, (now Chairman-Railway Board from August 23, 2017) who revived steam traction by the re-induction of the 1855-vintage Fairy Queen (EIR 22), the world's oldest steam locomotive in running condition. This loco used to haul a two-coach tourist train every winter from Delhi Cantonment to Alwar (in Rajasthan) and back, taking tourists to the Sariska Wild Life Sanctuary. This tour is well patronised by foreigners and Indians alike. After a theft of fixtures from this steam engine while parked at Delhi Cantonment station in March 2011, the engine was incapacitated. It was sent to Perambur Loco Works in Chennai (formerly Madras) for rehabilitation, with new parts fabricated for replacing the original fixtures; and the engine was back in shape again to haul special trains between Delhi Cantonment to Rewari and back in the winter of 2017.

NMR is the only rail line in peninsular India which still has steam engines, as the entire 119,630 kilometres (74,330 mi) network of Indian Railways has been progressively modernised by running trains on diesel or electric traction, and the steam engines have been phased out by the end of the year 1996. Several among these have been auctioned, broken to bits and sold as scrap-metal. The last broad gauge steam engine, a WL class loco no. 15005, named "Shere-e-Punjab," which was in use in the Ferozepur Division of Northern Railway, has found its place in the National Rail Museum, New Delhi. All over the railway network, narrow and metre gauge routes are progressively being converted to broad gauge under the 'project unigauge' scheme which was conceived over two decades ago. The Hill railways in India, however, still retain their original gauges.

The photographs in the book are mostly from my own collection of prints and colour slides. One of my photos depicting a rare view of the train on the rack section being pulled uphill with the engine at the front end instead of its normal position at the rear of the formation; was presented to the Station Master, Coonoor, T. Raveendranathan. It is prominently displayed in the office of the station master. The photograph was appreciated by the UNESCO team who assessed the heritage value of the Nilgiri Mountain Railway in September 2004. More recently, the members of the Swiss National Television who visited Coonoor in March 2007 to make a documentary film on this scenic mountain railway also appreciated the photograph, as per Station Master Saravana Kumar.

The first edition of my book was released on October 17, 2008 at a function held at the Coonoor Club, organised by the Nilgiris Cultural Association and the Nilgiri Mountain Railway Society; on the occasion of the Centenary of the Extension of the Nilgiri Mountain Railway from Coonoor to Ooty - this section was opened on October 15, 1908. A report on the book release was carried in the English daily, The Hindu, dated October 20, 2008, which can be read on this link:

http://www.thehindu.com/todays-paper/tp-national/tp-tamilnadu/
Role-of-local-people-in-keeping-NMR-alive-hailed/article15325432.ece

It is also a matter of pride that when Indian Railways released their first on-board magazine "Rail Bandhu" on May 16, 2011, for the reading pleasure of passengers in air-conditioned sleeper cars; it had a cover picture and lead story on the Nilgiri Mountain Railway (NMR), and my book was listed as a reference. A page on Reader's feedback and more photographs have been included in the revised edition because it would interest anyone who has travelled on this scenic line in the past; and if at all the railway slides into oblivion, this book would be of immense value to excite mystic chords of memory. Some people aboard a train toward Ootacamund want to experience the ride into the hills amidst the magnificent scenery, while others want to learn how the engineering skills of the bygone era had been harnessed in laying a railway line over steep mountainous terrain. Today, the metre gauge Nilgiri Mountain Railway and the narrow gauge Darjeeling Himalayan Railway are the only surviving steam operated routes on Indian Railways, and efforts to ensure the survival of steam engines in the interest of heritage and tourism is of utmost importance.

A senior official of Indian Railways, Mayank Tewari, who perused the first edition of my book commented, "Even though the need for this book is felt, the Railways need to grow up because it could not digest some of the criticism." In my view criticism acts as a catalyst for the Railways - to motivate them, and it is noteworthy that the railway authorities are heeding the voice of the public by initiating efforts to improve the operation of the now 118 years old NMR – the only rack railway in Asia; and sanctioning the manufacture of four new steam engines to replace the vintage Swiss engines. The Railways have risen to the occasion after the massive devastation to the track and bridges caused by torrential rain, landslides, and large chunks of rock dislodged from the hillside in November 2009. The work on re-building the track and bridges was accomplished in record time. This World Heritage mountain railway is a beautiful national asset and merits proper care and attention at all times to ensure its survival for posterity.

A page on Reader's feedback and more photographs was included in the revised edition in 2012 because it would interest anyone who has travelled on this scenic line in the past; and if at all the railway slides into oblivion, this book would be of immense historical value. In this edition, more details on latest developments on the Nilgiri line till the beginning of the year 2018 have been included to provide an updated view. Presently, the metre gauge Nilgiri Mountain Railway and the narrow gauge Darjeeling Himalayan Railway are the only surviving steam hauled routes on Indian Railways; and efforts to ensure the survival of steam engines in the interest of heritage and tourism is of utmost importance.

I am sure that this book would be of immense interest to all railway enthusiasts, particularly those who admire the Nilgiri Mountain Railway; and more than ever to those who have worked on this line, as it reflects the trials and tribulations of this railway in its struggle for survival.

It is now hoped that the government of India and its Ministry of Railways would do their bit to ensure that this scenic and unique railway would see better times with proper maintenance, procure new steam engines suitable to operate on the steep gradients on the line, and modernise it for efficient operation befitting its well earned World Heritage tag; more so because it is a major tourist attraction not only in India but the world over. Hordes of visitors, which includes foreigners, now visit the Nilgiri Hills just to travel by the NMR, but are at times left stranded as the train breaks down en route deep in the forests between Kallar and Coonoor owing to breakdown of the ageing Swiss steam engine.

**– V.M. Govind Krishnan**
**E-mail: vmgovindkrishnan@gmail.com**

# Introduction

There are seven mountain rail lines in India and each has an aura of its own. Four of these lines are located in the Himalayan range – to Darjeeling, Jogindernagar, Shimla, and Baramulla; one in western India to Matheran, and one in north-east India toward Agartala. The steepest of them all leads to the Victorian hill station of Ootacamund, in the Nilgiri Hills – derived from the vernacular *nila* (blue) *giri* (mountain) in Southern India, which is a part of the sprawling Western Ghats range of mountains.

Nilgiri Mountain Railway (NMR), everyone assumes is like the others – laid on narrow gauge tracks (width 2 ft. & 2 ft 6 in) In fact, it is a metre gauge line (width 3 ft 3 ⅜ in or 1000 mm), and the only one of its kind in India to run on a rack and pinion system to negotiate gradients as steep as 1 in 12.50 (i.e. 1 foot gain or loss for every 12.50 feet covered). This scenic 28 ½-mile (46 km) railway has only one parallel in the world – in distant Switzerland.

It is truly a marvel of engineering skill and it was conceived long before the ghat road to Ootacamund (or Ooty, and now officially known as Udagamandalam), came into existence. This railway links the plains at Mettupalayam with Coonoor (elevation 6000 ft.), which is a famous health resort with the Pasteur Institute of Southern India – a centre for preparing anti-rabies vaccine, a Silk Farm for sericulture, and the Sims Park - laid in 1874, with its varied flora and trees such as mahogany, birch, Burma teak, Spanish cherry and a lone conifer - brought from Australia, Canary Is., Venezuela, Chile, Mexico, Patagonia, Cape of Good Hope, and China. It is a botanist's delight. Located nearby are lush tea gardens, beautiful tourist spots, and waterfalls nearby such as the St. Catherine's falls, and the Law's falls – named after G.V. Law, who laid the 22-mile ghat road between Mettupalayam and Coonoor. Life in Coonoor oscillates between a dawdle and a doze, though the town now supports a population of around two lakhs and abounds in haphazardly constructed and unauthorised buildings amidst dwindling forest cover. A large number of polluting public vehicles blaring air horns, more in number than required in the hill towns congest the roads.

The railway then passes via Wellington - the seat of the Madras Regimental Center and the Defence Services Staff College, the Cordite factory at Aravankadu where explosives for the military is manufactured, the beautiful valley of Ketti, the quaint station at Lovedale near which is situated the famed Lawrence School. The line then passes alongside the long-closed station at Fernhill – now a bungalow for railway officers visiting the region, and the scenic Ooty Lake before it terminates at Ootacamund (elevation 7500 ft). Ooty is famous for the Government Botanical Garden, a Rose Garden, the annual horse races, and the 8640 ft. high Doddabetta peak. Nearby, the Mudumalai Wild Life Sanctuary on the highway to Mysore is well worth visiting, apart from other places of natural beauty surrounding this hill town, such as Kotagiri, Pykara waterfalls, Kundah, Glenmorgan, and the Mukurti Peak.

As is Coonoor, so is Ooty with its innumerable hotels in the name of tourism, and proliferating multi-storey constructions built with the connivance of corrupt officials of government agencies. Two decades ago, there was a ruling that no structure should be more than two-storey tall, and the top floor should have a gabled roof in keeping with the beauty of the surroundings. This rule is flouted with impunity in all the towns and villages in the Nilgiri Hills. Midsummer temperatures now soar to 30 deg. Celsius in both Ooty and Coonoor, as the microclimate has been altered. Water scarcity exists with the supply regulated every ten days or longer – unheard of three decades ago, due to lack of rains in the water-catchment areas, and because of silted reservoirs. However, the municipal authorities remain nonchalant.

## Environmental Degradation

The residents of the Nilgiris district have forgotten the meaning of the words, *"walking is a fashion in the hills"*. They now board the recently introduced mini buses and three-wheelers (autorickshaws), and the increasing number of private taxis – all of them increasing in number by leaps and bounds, proving to be a bane of the hills and a major source of noise, traffic congestion, and atmospheric pollution now prevalent in these towns. Extensive denudation of the forests and sholas, and other developmental activities during the past fifty years has disturbed the harmonious interaction between the flora and fauna and the tribal population living in the forests of the Nilgiris.

The hillsides of the Nilgiri range at altitudes of over 2500 metres are carpeted by deep mauve flowers of kurinji (strobilanthes acanthaceae), which bloom once every twelve years. In August 2006, kurunji had blossomed and the slopes above 2000 metres were carpeted with a spectacular bluish hue. The Department of Posts had issued a commemorative postage stamp on this flower in July 2006.

*"Earth has not anything to show more fair;*

*Dull would he be of soul who could pass by*

*A sight so touching in its majesty..."*

It is interesting to note that Ootacamund was first brought to the public eye by John Sullivan who was the Collector of Coimbatore in 1819. It later became the summer resort for the government personnel of the Madras Presidency. The British settlers found the place and its weather very similar to their own in England – the salubrious climate, rolling mist and sudden sporadic showers. Their government at Fort St. George, Madras, was duly notified, and Ooty in "the Neilgherries" was developed to suit their style of living with palatial buildings, large boarding schools, clubs, facilities for horse riding, horse racing, boating, and hunting. In those days, there was just a narrow path known as the "Hill Cart Road," to link the region with the plains, the only mode of transportation being a bullock cart – a long and slow trek through the hills. The subsequent construction of the metalled ghat road and the railway to Ooty made the access easy, but at the same time it made the destruction of the hills inevitable, by British greed and Indian complicity.

As said in the Outlook Traveller, "Hertfordshire lanes, Devonshire downs, Westmoreland lakes, Scotch trout and Lusitanian views..." that's what picture-perfect Ooty reminded Lord Lytton (Viceroy from 1876–1880) in the days of the Raj. Ooty reminds one of India's colonial past, with its single storey cottages, churches made of stone, peach and plum orchards and verdant greenery. Even today, the railway journey by the solitary "Nilagiri Passenger" enables the traveller to reminisce the British rule in India, as the train passes stations such as Adderley, Hillgrove, Runneymede, Wellington, Ketti, Lovedale, and the long closed Fernhill, while inhaling *"the cool, half-English Neilgherry air"* as the train winds its way to Ootacamund. The name of the train which used to be boldly displayed in English at the front of the last carriage has since the past few years become bilingual and new boards of smaller dimension depicts the name in Hindi and English, in keeping with the national policy. Now a Tamil equivalent has also appeared.

## Migrating Pachyderms and Other Sights

The Nilgiri range is home to a variety of flora and fauna, and a vast species of insects and butterflies. Around 3000 varieties of flowering plants, 74 species of mammals, 342 species of birds, several species of reptiles and amphibians have been identified. It's densely forested hills with lush greenery is a visual delight, though much of it has now been denuded due to political, and commercial considerations, and mindless development of the region in the name of tourism. This has altered the climatic condition of the entire Nilgiris district, so much so that the place is prone to drought and water scarcity these days. This is despite the region comprising the Nilgiris, and the forests of neighbouring states of Kerala and Karnataka being declared Nilgiri Biosphere Reserve (NBR) in 1986, an area of 5520 sq. kms.; with a view to preserve the ecological balance and the last of the tropical forests and rainforests in India. The Nilgiri range is a major water source for South India and its rivers serve three states, and their survival depends on it.

Many a time, on the Kallar - Adderley section of the railway, wild elephants cross the track. Incidentally, a sprawling school complex, Satchidananda Jothi Nikethan, has come up from 1996 onwards in about 45 acres of land carved out of the forest near Kallar; and the high power multi-strand electric fencing on its periphery has caused the death of some elephant calves. Incidentally this area falls in the migratory route of the pachyderms between the forests of Tamilnadu and Kerala, and environmentalists had opposed the construction of this school as elephants will forge new routes through other areas increasing man - animal conflict once the Kallar corridor becomes inaccessible. Currently, about 6000 elephants reside in the NBR, making it the largest continuous population of Asian elephants in the world.

Another interesting sight en route is at the now closed station at Adderley, where the loco crew has to assemble some pipes from a store room there, to enable them to fill water in the steam locomotive. These pipes are dismantled and stowed away before chugging along on its uphill journey. This is because thirsty wild elephants had damaged the pipes a few years ago. Occasionally, a herd of elephants prevent the movement of the train on the hill section, the journey is aborted and the train taken back to its starting point at Mettupalayam.

A perennial waterfall used to exist near Lamb's Rock which was visible for miles, long before one reached the base of the Nilgiri Hills, due to its free fall of about 200 feet. The waterfall has been wiped out following denudation of the area to create more tea gardens, and the consequent drying up of springs; the present sight being just a barren rocky face. Recently a cast iron currency chest built in with the station building at Kallar was unearthed. This was used to deposit the proceeds of the sale of tickets when the station was located amidst dense forest and the station master had to come and return by the same train, in the early days of the NMR. Even today, the station is in the forest though it has thinned out by deforestation, human settlements replacing the arecanut plantations, and encroachments on forest land in the area, due to population explosion.

So get aboard the Nilagiri Passenger at Mettupalayam and enjoy your leisurely crawl into the Nilgiri Hills, with the furiously huffing steam locomotive pushing the load of five carriages from the rear, the noise of the steaming pistons and clattering piston rods being enhanced inside the tunnels; and before long you will be enveloped in the moist and fluffy clouds, with mist and zero visibility, a perceptible drop in temperature with a nip in the air, and blessed perhaps by a shower or two on your ascent to Udagamandalam.

## Here's a Tip:

The best way to experience the fury of steam on the NMR is to take the train on the uphill run, and by being seated beside a window, but on the side opposite the platform at Mettupalayam, to obtain immense photographic opportunity as you go along, while listening to the music of the steam whistle, and the sound of the steam engine puffing along rhythmically with awesome determination, emitting dense plumes of smoke, at the rear end of the train. It is one of the greatest steam experiences still left in the world.

*Come, come along*

*Come with us, through tunnel long.*

*Follow the steep mountain track,*

*Listen to it chug,*

*Chug up the rack*

*Through fields of beetle nut*

*Tea plantations and funny little huts.*

*Don't worry you've nothing now to fear*

*'Cause you're on holiday here, So come, come along.*

# Early History

The Nilgiri Mountain Railway was opened for traffic only up to Coonoor from Mettupalayam on June 15, 1899, and was managed by a British firm, the Madras Railway Company, under an agreement with the Government of Madras. It was later extended to Ootacamund in October 1908.

The question of laying a railway up the Coonoor ghat from Mettupalayam (elevation 325.82 metres), the then terminus of the Madras Railway, was first mooted in 1854, long before the construction of the ghat road from Mettupalayam to Coonoor. In 1876 a Swiss engineer, Riggenbach, who was the inventor of the Rigi system of mountain railway, offered to construct the Nilgiri railway on Rigi lines, on standard gauge, and wanted the Government to give the land free of cost, and promise a guarantee of four per cent for ten years on the estimated cost of 400000 British Pounds; and grant tax exemption for the same period. The offer fell through as the Government could not agree to these terms.

In 1877 the Duke of Buckingham, the then governor of the Madras Presidency had estimates prepared for another project, providing for a railway line from Mettupalayam up to the base of the Nilgiri Hills near Kallar, at a distance of five miles, and then have an inclined ropeway of two miles up to Lady Canning's Seat – a popular picnic spot and tourist attraction near Coonoor – on a steep gradient of 1 ½ to 1, and another railway from the head of the ropeway to Coonoor, a distance of six miles. This scheme was costing approximately the same as Riggenbach's proposal, and due to the hazardous way of hauling passengers up an incline of 1 ½ to 1, this proposal was also dropped.

In 1882, Riggenbach returned to the Nilgiri Hills and prepared detailed estimates for a rack railway, which would cost only 132000 pounds. Major Morant of the Royal Engineers, the District Engineer of the Nilgiris, evinced great interest in the scheme. A company under the name 'The Nilgiri Railway Company Ltd' was formed to construct the line and the government gave it concessions in the matter of land acquisition, and in laying a railway line from Mettupalayam to Kallar, at a distance of five miles. The company requested the government to promise a guarantee of four percent on an outlay of 150000 pounds of about 20 years, but the government was not prepared to comply with this request without reciprocal conditions. Finally, an agreement was reached between the company and the Government of Madras, as a result of which a limited guarantee was promised by the latter.

The public in England was not satisfied with the nature of government guarantee or the estimates, and the company requested the government to modify its terms and a British engineer Richard Wooley was appointed to scrutinize the estimates. As the company could not afford to pay for his services, he offered to advance some money on the condition that he should be given the contract for the construction of the railway line. This offer was accepted, and in 1885, a new company, the Nilgiri Railway Co. was formed with a capital of Rs. 25 lakhs, and the proposal for a 'rack line' was dropped in favour of an 'adhesion line' at a gradient of 1 in 30 (a climb of 1 foot for every 30 feet of uphill travel), similar to the Darjeeling line. Eventually the rack system was decided upon, and, in 1886, a contract was entered between the Secretary of State for India, Government of Great Britain and the new company. In 1889, the capital required was raised in London, and in August 1891, Lord Wenlock, the then Governor of the Madras Presidency, cut the first sod of the line, and the railway construction began, and the track was to be a metre gauge (3 ft 3 ⅜ in or 1000 mm) line, worked on an ABT (alternate biting teeth) system, which was an improved modification of the Rigi rack-rail principle.

## First Train on Nilgiri Railway

A report in The Statesman, New Delhi, on August 7, 1994 in the column "100 years ago" reproduced a news item of August 7, 1894, which mentioned that "The first train on the Nilgiri Railway was successfully run from Mettapollium over the Bowani Bridge and as far as Kullar, the foot of the ghaut, on Thursday last, in the presence of Mr. Wightman, the chief engineer, and other officials of the Nilgiri and Madras Railways."

As ill luck would have it, the company could not complete the work and went into liquidation. Another company was formed in February 1896, and an agreement was signed between this company and the Secretary of State of India, whereby all land required was granted free along with a guarantee of three percent of the capital during the period of construction.

The railway was finally completed and opened for traffic on 15 June 1899 on the 27 kilometres (16 ¾ miles) route from Mettupalayam to Coonoor, which was the terminus for many years. The main facility for the upkeep and maintenance of the steam engines is located here, and remains functional to this day. The railway was operated by the Madras Railway Company under an agreement with the Government. Years later, it was taken over by the South Indian Railway (SIR) which subsequently changed to Southern Railway (SR) in 1952.

The Statesman, New Delhi, on Oct. 27, 1981 in the column "100 years ago," reproduced a news item dated October 27, 1881 which is shown here:

### The Nilgiri Railway

We learn that the authorities at Calcutta approve of the construction of the proposed line of railway on the Rigi system from Mettapollium to Coonoor, by the Nilgiri Railway Company, on the following conditions only, i.e. (1) a government guarantee of 4 per cent for five years from the date of through opening of the line which must be completed within three years of undertaking; (2) guarantee to be paid from provincial funds, as the line will serve only provincial interests and not form a proportion of the great railway system of India; (3) the guarantee must be in rupees and not in sterling money; (4) arrangements must be made for the conveyance of Government mails, soldiers, police and treasure at special reduced rates; (5) one mixed train, at least, must run daily in each direction; (6) that fare be at the discretion of the Company but within a maximum fixed by Government; (7) that Government be permitted to purchase the line at intervals of 10 years or other periods that may be fixed upon by the local Government; (8) that Government be reimbursed and all the profits earned in excess of 5 per cent, interest meanwhile being calculated at 4 per cent simple interest. Government will provide the land required by the Company for way and works. If these terms are agreed upon, a contract upon their bases will be drawn up between the Company and Government – Madras Times.

In January 1903, the government bought this line for Rs. 35 lakhs, and the Madras Railway Company continued to manage this railway on behalf of the government for a long time till the South Indian Railway Company purchased it in 1907. The line was extended from Coonoor to Ootacamund on the same gauge and over a distance of 19 km (11 ¾ miles) at a cost of Rs. 2440000, and was opened for traffic on October 15, 1908. Fernhill was the highest station on the route, from where the track gradually descended to Ootacamund, about three kilometres away - the elevation at the station being 7228 feet above Mean Sea Level.

Even before the line was laid up to Ooty in 1908, plans were being made to electrify the entire track, and also the towns of Ootacamund, Wellington and Coonoor. An estimate for Rs. 3129000 was submitted. As the cost was considered to be too much, the proposal was shelved.

Shown here is a news report from "The Times Archives" dated July 2, 1906, which was published in The Times of India, Bombay, on July 31, 1993:

**The Nilgiri Railway Electrification Scheme**

Madras, June 30: The government of India still has the question of the electrification of the Nilgiri railway, under consideration and even if the question were decided at once it would be impossible to finish the power stations in time for opening of the Coonoor - Ootacamund extension. Accordingly, for the first few months at any rate, the railway will be worked by steam. Work on that station is proceeding rapidly and though the stations on it will not be completed by then the authorities hope to have trains running by the end of May next.

It is believed that there is no doubt that the Government of India will consent to the working of the railway by electricity, it being only a question of finance – whether the profits of the railway will be enough to pay for constructing electrical works. If the scheme before the government is accepted, water power will come from the Coonoor River and from the Karliary, the water at the latter place being used again after it comes from the cordite factory in Coonoor. A river and a lake will be made at Wellington to give the necessary head of water. The question of using electricity to light Ootacamund, Coonoor and Wellington is also being considered, the only question being whether the supply of water, if used night and day, will be sufficient.

**The Nilgiris Gazetteer** published by W. Francis, ICS, in 1908 records: "The only railway in the district is that which runs from the terminus of the Madras Railway at Mettupalayam up the ghat to Coonoor. It is 16.9 miles long and is on meter gauge. It is now being extended to Ootacamund. The question of working the whole line by electric power is under consideration."

In later years, though this proposal came up from time to time, electric traction on the Nilgiri Mountain Railway never materialised.

# The Track

The railway line is 46 km (28 ½ miles) in length and starts from Mettupalayam, at an elevation of 1070 ft., to Ootacamund, at an elevation of 7228 ft. The track width is 1000 mm (3 ft 3 ⅜ in) i.e. metre gauge. The gradient on the line is maximum 1 in 40 up to Kallar from where the steep rack section begins till Coonoor. The maximum gradient on the rack railway is 1 in 12.28, and thence to Ooty at a gradient of max 1 in 23. The highest point on the line is at Fernhill near Ootacamund, at 7300 ft.

The line operates on ABT (alternate biting teeth) technology whereby centrally laid rack bars engage cog wheels under the locomotives and carriages. The rack bars are laid on cast iron chairs in a double row of about 1 ¾ inches apart and over 2 inches above the level of the guide rails so that the tooth of one rack is exactly opposite the gap of the other to ensure that the engine pinions do not work off the racks on the sharp curves. The rack bars were originally imported from England, but are now made locally at the Southern Railway's workshop. Special rack tongues facilitate the entry into the rack section.

Many of the sharp curves have curve lubricators (made in England) fitted on the track, to suitably grease them as the wheels pass by. Most of the curves are as sharp as 17.5 degrees, and the sharpest curves are located between Kallar and Coonoor. Almost all the lubricators are rusted and cannot be used today, and they have not been replaced a new.

The gradient on the 20 km (12 ¾ miles) section of the line from Kallar to Coonoor is very steep (mostly on a gradient of 1 in 12.50), and the track climbs continuously to 4363 ft. Due to the sloping track, even if the train stands with all its wheel-brakes fully applied, there is a possibility of the entire train sliding down. This explains the provision of toothed rack bars in between the guide rails, and these engage the pinion wheels fitted under the locomotive and the carriages and prevent the train from slipping.

The rack section of the railway ends at Coonoor, where the station is situated at an elevation of 5616 ft. above MSL. As the 19 km (11 ¾ miles) section of the line between Coonoor and Ootacamund is on a milder gradient, the steepest being 1 in 23, but mostly on a gradient of 1 in 30, the centrally laid rack bars are not seen on this section, and the train runs at a faster clip.

There are sixteen tunnels on the entire route, of which thirteen tunnels lie between Kallar and Coonoor - most of them unlined and in excellent condition. Tunnel No 7 opens directly on to a bridge, and is a wonderful sight en route. The longest tunnel is 317 feet, and spring water seeps into few of these tunnels from the rocky roof and sides.

The rails were originally procured from England. Some of these, manufactured in 1925 by Glenfield and Kilmarnock, Scotland, and imported in the 1950s are still in use on the main line today.

Trains are operated on the Absolute Block System with semaphore signals. A metallic ball placed in a special pocket in a large bamboo ring is exchanged at every station by the engine crew. The vintage equipment for train operations using the Neale's ball token machines at the stations is maintained in excellent condition, and is in use even now.

Some of the semaphore signal posts erected by the British have been replaced, while some others have been relocated farther away from the station, rather illogically locating the outer signals a kilometer away, almost half way between two stations in some places! The original signal-cabin at Coonoor was demolished over four decades ago and a new one was erected a few metres away, with better equipment and hand-operated levers. At all other stations en route, the signalling equipment remains unchanged. A suspended bit of rail and a hammer which served as the station's bell for ages has given way to the electric bell at Coonoor and Ooty, since the past few years. Other than such minor changes, the basic heritage structures remain unchanged. Also at Coonoor, a second platform has been built in mid 2007.

Some of the bridges are works of art, notably the curved bridge at Kallar with its tall stone piers and masonry arches; and the railway bridge at Wellington – the highest bridge on the NMR, with its stone piers supporting specially designed girders for the gradient on the track. There are thirty two major bridges on the entire route, many of them being curved structures and a visual delight, providing a good photo-op from a vantage window seat.

The journey through the densely forested hills via precipitous slopes, precariously overhanging boulders and moss laden rocky terrain with abundant waterfalls, presents stunning scenery and is a photographer's delight. The maximum speed on the non-rack section is thirty kilometres per hour, and it is only thirteen kilometers per hour on the steep rack and pinion route between Kallar and Coonoor. Hence travellers on the route need feel no altitude sickness or nausea as the train climbs slowly into the Nilgiri Hills.

At a point between Adderley and Hillgrove stations, the train passes below a huge rocky mass of granite projecting over the track on a precipitous terrain (erroneously termed "half tunnel" by the local populace).

A proper view of this can only be seen from the leading compartment of the train as it heads towards Coonoor, since from the other carriages one may miss the scene altogether.

Said a railway enthusiast:

*Any number of plane journeys*

*Cannot make up for*

*The excitement and romance*

*Of a single ride on*

*The Indian Railways*

# The Rolling Stock

## The Locomotives

The earliest steam engines used on the line were the R class rack and adhesion locos built in 1897 by Beyer, Peacock and Co. in Manchester. Each 2–4–0 type engine weighed 33 tons 14 cwt. They were subsequently replaced by more efficient engines specially built for use on the steep gradients on this line. The ones presently in use were obtained in 1925 and 1952. These complicated engines were built at Winterthur, Switzerland, by SLM - Swiss Locomotive & Machine Works (Schweizerische Lokomotiv und Maschinenfabrik). Each of these X class locos weighed 48 tons, and is of the 4-cylinder compound type wherein two low pressure cylinders drove the pinion wheels and two high pressure cylinders drove the adhesion wheels. Steam acts through a separate set of cylinders driving a special crank shaft connected by spur gearing with the axle carrying the toothed wheel. The spur wheels are in duplicate so that even if one is damaged, the other is strong enough to do the work.

A mechanism has been provided to shut off the low pressure cylinders when operating on the non-rack section and this noisy changeover is best viewed on the uphill run of the train as it nears the level crossing gates at Coonoor where the rack section of this railway ends.

Each of these 0–8–2 type X class steam engines had a tender capacity of 1200 gallons. A sand hump is located on the boiler from which copper tubes lead to the adhesion wheels. Fine sand is sprayed on the track to facilitate adhesion in wet conditions, on the uphill journey. As the train moved on the rack section, oil is forced by steam pressure through a pipe on to the pinions and thereby to the rack bars to grease them.

One of these 1952-vintage coal burning locos, no. X-37395, was successfully converted to oil firing in the year 2002, and had been in active service on the Mettupalayam to Coonoor section. The modification had boosted the pushing (not pulling) power of the ancient steam engine, and it was capable of hauling trains with better efficiency, and was reportedly 'less polluting' to the environment.

An earlier attempt to convert a steam loco no. X-37390 failed and this engine lay unused on a siding at Coonoor for several months. It was declared 'unserviceable', and has been mounted on a platform outside the Coonoor railway station, and unveiled on the Centenary Day of the NMR on June 15, 1999. This Swiss steam engine was built in 1922 and had logged 7.5 lakh km in its 75 years of service from Oct 1923, as per the engraved stone plaque erected alongside.

Two more old steam engines were converted in 2007 from coal burner to oil firing mode at the Golden Rock Workshop of the Railways at Tiruchirappally. One of these, engine no. X-37391 was commissioned to haul trains in Oct. 2007, and one more was undergoing trials.

By the end of 2017, just two vintage steam engines built in Winterthur, Switzerland, and converted to oil firing in recent times, remain operational on the rack railway route, while the rest have been withdrawn from service and mounted at displays at various locations in the Indian state of Tamilnadu. Four new oil fired steam engines reportedly built from scratch, based on original designs with Golden Rock Workshop of the Railways, are in use on the line today – and these entered service between 2011 and 2014.

## Loco Shed, Coonoor

The few Swiss-built steam engines left on the NMR are over aged and nearing the end of their active lives, and such engines are out of production. The Loco Shed at Coonoor is the centre for maintaining these Swiss beauties right from the inception of the Nilgiri Railway. A quaint vintage hand-operated crane parked at the loco shed is in use to this day. It was manufactured in 1886 by Cowans Sheldon and Co. Ltd., Carlisle, England. Many a time one can see the steam engines stripped to a mere skeleton for a major overhaul, and a few days hence, they are back in action.

## The Carriages

The carriages and freight wagons were mostly built in 1914 by the Birmingham Railway Carriage and Wagon Company Ltd, Smethwick, England. Some were made by Waggonlits, Germany, and some were sourced from Gloucester in England. The earlier wooden carriages had coil springs in the primary suspension and laminated bearing leaf springs in the secondary suspension. Rolled up canvas sheets covered its wide windows, which were let down in case of rain. Oil lamps were inserted from special slots on the roof to provide a dim glow inside the carriage. As all the carriages have been reconditioned in the 1960s, they sport heavy wooden frames and glass shutters, and electric lighting was introduced by having a battery pack in the goods wagon of the train. As a consequence the carriages became heavier than before, and proved to be a strain on the ageing steam engines.

Every carriage – whether for passengers or freight, has a verandah at the rear with a brakesman in uniform, to independently operate levers for the brakes and the cog wheels. As some of the carriages were used to transport military personnel, the wooden benches could be lifted to place their rifles in the slots below.

The carriages have been remodeled again during 1995–96, and twelve special coaches were reconstructed on the original chassis, with transparent polycarbonate roofing to maximise lighting, and wider windows to enable the passengers to have a better view of the scenic beauty of the hilly region. However, due to lesser leg room, the carriages became more cramped despite the contoured plastic seats, which replaced the earlier wooden benches. The transparent roofing has since been changed due to intense heating of the carriages due to bright sunlight and heat penetrating from above.

## Special Freight Wagons

Specially built carriages (Horse Float), were used to transport race horses for the Ootacamund Races held every year in the summer season, and explosives from the Cordite factory at Aravankadu was transported in white-painted freight wagons marked 'Explosives'. Open wagons were used for coal and timber, and closed wagons for tea and other cargoes.

## A Primitive, Yet Precise Drill

En route uphill, the engine pushes the rake (load of carriages) from the rear. As the driver is blind to the track ahead, the leading brakesman with flags signals the "all clear" to the following carriage. All brakesmen relay the flag signal till it is seen by the driver, who acknowledges it with a shrill blast of the loco whistle. This primitive drill executed with great precision, reveals the discipline on this line.

The Last Vehicle (LV) sign is displayed on the locomotive on the uphill run. On the downhill run, the engine hauls the train in reverse gear, and the driver has a clear view of the track in front.

## A Mandatory Check

The fireman gets down peering under the loco to ensure proper alignment of the cog wheels below the engine to the rack rails when the train enters the rack section between Coonoor and Kallar, on both the uphill and downhill runs on the steep incline.

Children used to squeal in delight, and honeymooners cuddled each other as the train chugged through the dark and eerie tunnels. Nowadays, their joy has diminished to a great extent as the Guard switches on the electric lights in the carriages before the train enters the tunnels.

# Official Indifference & Public Opinion

### Dismantling of Nilagiri Railway Proposed By the Union Government

In January 1968, the daily newspapers reported that the Union Government proposed to dismantle the Nilgiri Mountain Railway (NMR), on the plea that it was uneconomic. However, at that time, no effort was made by them to improve the condition of the line and its operation. This proposal sparked a series of protests by various sections of the public, and was highlighted by the media, as the lifeline to the Nilgiri Hills was under threat of closure.

The Weekly Mail of January 27, 1968 in their report "Case against the closure of Nilgiris Railway" said, "The proposal of the Union Government to close down the Nilgiris Mountain Railway due to sheer uneconomic reasons has come as a shock. Even before the road transport was conceived the railway came into being, and for the past sixty years, the railway has been doing yeoman service to the people."

On a query to the Ministry of Railways, government of India, at New Delhi, a reply was received dated January 18, 1969 from S. V. Ramasubban of the Railway Board stating, "With reference to your letter dated 21.12.68 addressed to the Minister for Railways, I am directed to state that no final decision in regard to the closure of the Mettupalayam-Ootacamund line has been taken. I am directed to assure you that all relevant factors will be taken into account before a final decision is taken in regard to closure of this line."

### The Indian Express of August 6, 1971, reports from Coimbatore:

### Neglected Rail Line

"The Nilgiris mountain railway, one of the tourist attractions of the state, may have to be scrapped because of official indifference. The 30 mile track rail, connecting Mettupalayam to Ooty, the queen among hill stations, is one of the lines the railway administration wanted to scrap on ground of being 'uneconomic' But instead of improving the service to make the line remunerative and attractive to traffic things are being done to create a situation to make the scrapping of the mountain line 'inevitable', according to well-informed sources." The report further states "It is also stated that the mountain rails laid in 1891 have already developed cracks, which is a safety hazard. After persistent pleas by the Engineering Department, a sum of Rs. 66000 was sanctioned for improving the track, for purchase of sleepers and rails." It was also reported that "There has also been a systematic reduction of staff in the name of economy. About six posts of Assistant Station Master have been surrendered at Ooty, Ketti, Wellington, Coonoor, Runneymede and Adderley, increasing the workload of the remaining staff. There should be one brakesman in every carriage for safety reason in the mountain railway and 36 brakes-men out of a total of 64 have already been dispensed with. All these things have created a genuine doubt about the future of the Nilgiris mountain railway."

To my letter addressed to the Union Minister for Railways, K. Hanumanthaiya, on September 12, 1971, two replies were received.

The first was from R.K. Dhawan, Addl. Private Secretary to the Minister, whose letter of Sep. 21, 1971 merely acknowledged the receipt of the letter sent to the Minister, and the other was dated January 2, 1972, from V.P. Sawhney, Secretary in the Ministry of Railways who specified: "There was no proposal under consideration to close down this branch line though investigations are on hand to minimise the working expenses of this line in view of the continuous loss in working." The letter also said that "The dieselisation of Nilgiri Mountain Railway has also been examined but was not found to be economical. The existing steam locos operating on the section are considered to be in a satisfactory condition and do not require replacement."

### Student-Police Clash: Ooty Station Incident

On October 4, 1971, the Ootacamund railway station was the scene of an untoward incident when the Nilagiri Express arrived at about 1.55 P.M. A party of 60 students from Govind Ballabh Pant Polytechnic, New Delhi, was aboard the train, led by two lecturers and two instructors. At Ketti station on NMR, one of the students who had disembarked was left behind as the train moved off, and the Guard refused to halt the train, perhaps because it was running behind time by almost two hours. Tension mounted by the time the train reached the next station, Lovedale, as the students manhandled the railway staff. At Ootacamund, the train was received by a large posse of police constables and security men. The Nilgiris Collector, J. Shivakumar along with T.D. Krishnamurthy, Deputy Suptd. Police and a contingent of armed police reached the station and quelled the riot. This was reported in the daily, The Hindu, on the following day.

In those days, steam traction out of Madras was being phased out, and the Madras Central to Mettupalayam Nilagiri Express (on broad gauge tracks) used to be hauled by a WDM class diesel engine till Erode, from where a WP class bullet-nose steam locomotive hauled the train to Mettupalayam. Whatever time was gained on the first segment was lost in the second, due to the ageing steam engine used for this "Express train". So, on most days the train reached Mettupalayam later than scheduled, and since the hill train to Ootacamund was its only connection, it was also consequently delayed. Later, electric engines hauled trains till Coimbatore from where a diesel engine took over since the branch line to Mettupalayam was not electrified, but the train maintained its schedule. From July 3, 2015 the Nilagiri Express is hauled by a WAP-7 electric engine on the entire route to Mettupalayam and back to Madras (now Chennai).

On March 9, 1972, The Hindu, Madras, published a letter by P.S. Subramaniam, President, Tamil Nadu Railway Users' Chamber, excerpts from which are reproduced here:

"It should be found out whether an 'uneconomic' line could be made 'economic' by adopting certain measures of operational efficiency and by introducing essential passenger amenities. The Nilgiri hill railway may be taken as a case in point. According to the Railway Board, the loss incurred on this sector is between Rs. 23 and Rs. 26 lakhs. This railway built by Swiss engineers, regarded as one of the best tourist attractions in Southern India and has seen no improvements in the last sixty years. After making on-the-spot enquiries, we are convinced that this uneconomic line could be rendered economic." The letter is reproduced in full in the final section of the book.

Heavy rains caused landslides between Adderley and Hillgrove stations on the NMR on December 7, 1972. While about 150 workers were clearing the debris, another landslip occurred at the same spot burying ten workers. The authorities could not reach the spot to save the workers due to continuous torrential rain. The track, buried under a mound of earth, was cleared and train service was resumed from January 5, 1973.

## A Seven-Month Stoppage of NMR Trains

The train services were suspended indefinitely from December 1973 sparking a series of protests from the public. Letters came to various newspapers from far and wide. One such letter by Vinod Chhabra, from Albany, New York, USA, in The Hindu on May 1, 1974, urging the authorities to restore the train services, reads, "The decision to scrap this train service between Mettupalayam and Ootacamund is catastrophic. At a time when the Indian economy is cracking under the skyrocketing imported oil prices, it is distressing to learn that the railway ministry has done away with the cheaper coal-based mode of transportation."

A Jesuit priest, Fr. H. Pinto, from Loyola College, Madras, wrote to me that a deputation waited on the Governor in Ootacamund asking for the restoration of the train service, and that there was an agitation in favour of resumption of trains on the Nilgiri Mountain Railway.

The Indian Express, Madras, dated April 20, 1974 reporting on the suspension of trains hitting tourist traffic to Ooty said, "Suspension of train services from Mettupalayam to Ootacamund because of coal shortage for over four months has hit hard the tourist traffic to the Nilgiris. The season has commenced here and many tourists have been denied of the pleasure to travel in this mountain railway. The slogan 'Travel by train, enjoy beauty and save money' put up by railway authorities at every station has become a misnomer. When the railway administration is running trains to other hill stations, reason for suspending services on the Nilgiri Mountain Railway is beyond anybody's comprehension, and it is feared that suspension of the train services may be a prelude to dismantling of the railway link. "People hope that both the railway and tourism ministers at the Centre will come to the rescue and do needful in restoring train services so that tourist traffic is not jeopardised."

My query to the General Manager, Southern Railway elicited a reply dated May 27, 1974 stating, "Due to critical coal position on this Railway train services on a number of sections, including the Mettupalayam - Ootacamund section, have been cancelled. Further, a strike by certain sections of railway staff made the position difficult. However the matter will be reviewed after the position becomes normal."

Finally, on July 5, 1974, trains commenced running between Coonoor and Ootacamund, and from July 15th, the services were restored between Coonoor and Mettupalayam, after a period of seven months of cancellation.

The Mail, Madras, dated August 31, 1974 published three alternative proposals to the minister for railways, L.N. Mishra, from the Tamilnadu chief minister, M. Karunanidhi. They were a) The centre should reopen the "uneconomic line," b) The state government should be allowed to operate it if the centre cannot revive it, and c) the line can be operated jointly by the centre and the state government.

A report in The Statesman, New Delhi of July 24, 1975 mentioned that G.S.A. Saldanha, general manager of Southern Railway said, "It was doubtless a very uneconomical line, but a policy decision had been taken not to scrap it."

The Statesman of June 2, 1976 in the article "Reprieve for a Dream Railway" mentioned that "The public is palpably fond of this dream railway. It is amazing, say many, that officialdom should at all consider dismantling what would be considered a proud national asset and a first class tourist attraction anywhere else in the world."

## Southern Railway Time Tables

It is interesting to sneak a quick look at the Southern Railway time-tables. In April 1966, the time taken for the uphill runs of the 36 Down Nilagiri Express (or Blue Mountain Express) from Mettupalayam to Ootacamund was 3 hrs 55 min. The trains used to have six carriages (its maximum limit) and one of these was a goods wagon to carry cargo and excess luggage. There used to be three pairs of trains on the entire route each way, besides two more pairs each way daily between Coonoor and Ootacamund. The 35 Up Nilagiri Express from Ooty to Mettupalayam covered the distance in 3 hrs 40 min.

In April 1977, the published time taken for the uphill journey increased to 4 hrs 25 min, and in April 1981 it further increased to 4 hrs 40 min, with a change of steam engine at Coonoor. This was because some of the engines maintained by the loco shed at Coonoor became unfit for the rack and pinion section of the railway, and could therefore be run only on the non-rack section from Coonoor to Ooty. To make use of these engines, the change of engine at Coonoor was introduced. The frequency of the trains was also reduced, along with a reduction in the number of carriages as the engines could not haul the full load of six carriages. The downhill time remained constant, as the engine pulls the rake effortlessly in reverse gear, but the 'vehicle limit' was reduced from six to five.

Presently it takes five hours – at times even longer, to cover the 46 km distance on the uphill run with a change from steam engine to a YDM-4 diesel engine at Coonoor, because the vintage steam engines in use have lost their pushing (not pulling) power, and are prone to breakdown en route. The diesel engine was first introduced on this railway in April 1993 for operating trains on the Coonoor to Ootacamund (Udagamandalam) section only. One more diesel engine was brought in March 1998 to operate more trains between Coonoor and Ooty.

## Cannibalising of Parts

Another reason for this deteriorating situation is said to be the cannibalising of parts due to unavailability of spares. Hence some usable parts from older steam engines, mainly the rack and pinion mechanism and its accessories, were transferred to others to keep them in running condition, thus enabling the NMR to operate train services between Mettupalayam and Coonoor, till such time new engines were procured to replace them.

However, as a consequence the number of locomotives fit to operate on the steep rack and pinion route registered a decrease. There were fourteen steam engines in 1972, which have reduced to about five as in 2006. All the Swiss built steam engines are maintained by the loco shed at Coonoor. One can see the engines being dismantled, repaired and assembled again with the help of an ancient hand operated crane parked on the embankment alongside. Complete overhaul of the vintage locos is done here, right from the inception of this railway, as Coonoor used to be the terminus of the Nilgiri Railway for many years, till the time the line was extended to Ootacamund in 1908.

The maximum vehicle limit was six carriages, but nowadays the trains are operated with a maximum of four or five carriages. On rather rare occasions, one can see a carriage turned around so that the verandahs with the levers for brakes and rack-bars of two carriages face each other to be operated by one brakesman, perhaps due to shortage of manpower! For safety reasons on this line it is mandatory to have a brakesman in every carriage.

And so it goes:

*For want of maintenance,*
*Speed was lost.*
*For want of speed,*
*Efficiency was lost.*
*For want of efficiency,*
*Progress was lost.*

## Disruption and Coal Shortage

Land slips following continuous and heavy rains in the Nilgiris district blocked the track between Mettupalayam and Ootacamund and train services remained suspended from since the beginning of November 1977. The track was cleared of the mounds of earth in about a fortnight, but train services could not be restored for want of coal. Finally, around mid December 1977 the train services resumed after reports of the stoppage were published in the daily newspapers.

Arthur Zich, in his article "India's 60000-kilometre lifeline" (Reader's Digest, Dec. 1978) described his travel on the NMR:

## Spectacular Journey

"My first experience on India's railways was a journey up the precipitous face of the Nilgiri Mountains from Mettupalaiyam to Ootacamund, the fabled "Queen of the Hill Stations". A four-hour, 45 kilometre crawl, the trip offered spectacular views of the coastal plains and some heart-stopping halts atop trestles stretching over seemingly bottomless gorges."

Landslips caused by heavy rains obstructed and damaged the mountain track, and train services on the NMR remained suspended from November 1979 onwards.

On February 5, 1980, the following news report was seen in The Hindu:

## Train Service to Be Resumed

Madras, Feb 4: The Udhagamandalam – Mettupalayam Nilgiri Express will be resumed from February 7. Train services on this section were suspended in November last following landslips. The operation of the mixed passenger train between these two stations will be notified later, according to Southern Railway authorities.

## Agitation for NMR by Southern Railway Employees Sangh

Trains on the NMR were suspended again from June 11, 1981 due to coal shortage, and restored from June 24, 1981 after the media highlighted this.

Meanwhile, the Southern Railway Employees Sangh (SRES), Perambur, had a long agitation followed by a meeting at Coonoor, as there was a threat to the survival of this unique railway. The Sangh called "for the modernisation of the line and maintaining the twelve X class locos in fit condition and to operate the train service on the entire route in a satisfactory manner duly giving equal importance as that of train services in the other sections and not to kill the sick baby."

## Boulder Hits Train

On August 6, 1981, a boulder rolled down and hit the guard's compartment of the Nilagiri Express as it was chugging along towards Coonoor on the Kallar - Hillgrove ghat section injuring the guard and three others, and killing a gang-man who was patrolling the track.

## First Accident in Living Memory on Nilgiri Railway

On February 21, 1982, a major mishap occurred on the hill section between Adderley and Hillgrove stations when a goods train proceeding uphill from Mettupalayam, carrying coal to the loco shed at Coonoor, mysteriously slid downhill and fell off a bridge over a curve into a deep ravine, killing all eight persons aboard including the engine driver and the fireman. Hence, the cause of the mishap remains unclear. It is presumed that a failure of the brake system may have been the cause of the mishap. Incidentally this was the first accident in living memory on this line. The steam engine involved in this mishap was X-37385.

The Hindu, Madras, reported on February 22, 1982 that M.P. Sastry, Commissioner of Railway Safety, Southern Circle will hold an inquiry into the goods train accident in the Nilgiris ghat section. It also reported that the Union Minister of State for railways, C.K. Jaffer Sharief "could not visit the accident spot as he developed cramps and felt sick while going round Mettupalayam to see the victims' families. He therefore returned to Coimbatore after visiting Kallar where he inspected the mountain railway track and heard from officials how the unique 'rack and pinion system' worked." The report also said that "Mr. Sharief said a committee of experts had been asked to go into all aspects of the working of the mountain railway, and its future will be decided on the basis of its recommendations." He also said that "The locos on this system were 52 years old and with the financial constraints now, it would not be possible to replace them." The minister, Jaffer Sharief, is said to have remarked, "Do you want safe travel or the mountain railway?"

As per the railway official accompanying the minister C.K. Jaffer Sharief, the engine was quite old and its haulage capacity had been reduced, but its operation could not be considered unsafe. He also said that the load carried was within permissible limits. However, the findings of the inquiry conducted have not been made known, but all train services on this 46-kilometer line remained cancelled for months at a stretch.

This brings to my mind a skit from Khushwant Singh's column, "With malice towards one and all" in The Hindustan Times, New Delhi dated October 7, 1995:

*A Railway Minister named Sharief*

*Brought many a family to grief;*

*With late running so frequent*

*Plus a monthly accident –*

*Oh, how one wishes his reign was brief!*

*(Courtesy Prabhat S.Vaidya, Bombay)*


**Excerpts from a report in The Indian Express, Madurai, April 12, 1982:**


## Ooty Season Begins

Ootacamund, April 11: The season has already commenced! Visitors are pouring in from all parts of the country. For the races commencing on April 14, all concerned with it – and race goers are expected to be here in time.

While there is much talk and publicity for attracting tourists to this Queen of hill stations, there is no rail service from Mettupalayam to Ootacamund for the past two months after the goods train accident between Adderley and Hill Grove on the Mettupalayam – Ootacamund railway. The railway authorities have suspended the train service and repairs to the track are going on.

But the railway authorities here are reluctant to say when the line will be ready for resuming the train service from Mettupalayam to Ootacamund. Many tourists desire to travel only by train to see and enjoy the panoramic view on the ghat section and some do not like bus journey. As such the importance of resuming the train service as quickly as possible is felt by the commuters.

The Railway authorities should make all efforts to repair the damaged track and resume the train service. If train service is not resumed early, it will hit the tourist traffic very much.

The Indian Express, dated Thursday, April 29, 1982 reported:

## Diesel Traction for Nilgiris Hill Railway

Madras, Wed. April 28: Train services on the Mettupalayam-Coonoor section of the mountain railway are likely to be restored with diesel traction in two or three months' time.

A team of Swiss experts are coming next month to inspect this unique section where trains were operated with a rack and pinion system, Mr. Verghese Anver, General Manager, Southern Railway disclosed on Tuesday.

## Public Angst on the Withdrawal of Train Service

Public protest followed since train services remained cancelled for months at a stretch following the goods train derailment on Feb. 21, 1982, as there was apprehension regarding the permanent closure of this mountain railway.

My letter to the railway authorities on March 3, 1982 pointed out: "It is well known that the vintage Swiss-built steam locos (some over 50 years old) have lost their efficiency. The mountain track and rack rails need replacement, and the rolling stock need overhauling; but these urgent needs are shelved in the name of economy and to provide a case for uneconomic operation of the line and allow it to die."

A concerned citizen, M. Thomas from New Delhi said, "To argue that the railway is of sentimental value and merely a tourist attraction, and that in spite of being uneconomic it is being run for these reasons, is one-sided and ill informed reasoning. The argument must not confine itself to tourism of economic viability. The question of communication and transport from the plains to the Nilgiris is a part of the entire development strategy for the ghats and is intimately associated with its economy and ecology. The question of continuance of the railway must be reviewed from this aspect."

K. Kallan, a Member of the Legislative Assembly said, "The reported remarks of the Minister of State for railways, C.K. Jaffer Sharief on the future of the Nilgiri Mountain Railway have caused genuine apprehension in the minds of the people in the Nilgiris. This railway is an engineering marvel and a rich legacy left by the British and serves as a vital alternative mode of transport to the Nilgiri Hills. As such, the railway administration instead of repeatedly stating that it is uneconomical should take positive steps to improve its working to make it not only economical but also profitable."

## Passenger Trains Restored, But Freight Trains Withdrawn

Finally, the trains were resumed from May 1, 1982 between Coonoor and Ootacamund. The Mettupalayam-Coonoor rack section was opened to traffic from October 2, 1982 – after seven months of closure - but with just one pair of trains, the Nilagiri Passenger (formerly 'Nilagiri Express') to connect the Nilagiri Expresses to/from Madras Central, at Mettupalayam.

Three pairs of trains used to operate between Ootacamund and Mettupalayam in 1966, two pairs prior to the mishap in Feb. 1982, and now it is just one pair, with reduction in the carrying capacity, as number of carriages was reduced from six to three or four. Goods trains, which were quite frequently operating, carrying cargoes of tea, vegetables, timber and ammunition from the Cordite factory at Aravankadu, ceased to run, and these cargo loads were sent by road. The Madras Regimental Centre also closed down their freight operations at Wellington station, as army trucks served the purpose. Only goods and materials for the NMR were being brought by a goods train. Freight carried on the NMR used to be a good source of revenue, as per Mendez, a goods booking official at the Coonoor station many years ago, during the heyday of the Nilgiri Railway.

## Official Explanation on the Accident

Meanwhile, the official inquiry committee which went into the cause of the goods train accident on Feb. 21, 1982, advised that extra care was needed for its maintenance as "a stage has been reached when this becomes a runaway situation and normal maintenance efforts are not able to overtake and stem the deteriorating tide."

## Nilagiri Express to Nilagiri Passenger

Owing to the change in nomenclature of the hill train from "Express" to "Passenger," the fare also reduced a bit. Also, in order to wean away travellers from road travel to rail travel, fares on this section viz. Mettupalayam – Coonoor - Udagamandalam, were kept a stage lower than the normal bus fares, and hoardings proclaiming this change were displayed on the roadside. This move, though it generated some crowd, did not rake in revenue, as the train service was deemed to be unreliable and prone to sudden cancellations.

## Closure of stations on Nilgiri Railway

As train crossings at intermediate stations en route were past memories due to a solitary passenger train operating each way on the scenic ghat section between Mettupalayam and Coonoor, the stations on the line were progressively closed, notably Kallar, Adderley, Runneymede, and Katery Road. Only Hillgrove station was functional, with the station master commuting by road from the plains up to a wayside village, Burliar, and trudging up a steep forest path to man the station before the arrival of the train. He used to return in the evening by the train going to Mettupalayam. The cottage for the station master and the gangmen quarters near the Adderley station were "abandoned," and fell into disuse.

The station at Fernhill at the outskirts of Ooty was closed in the 1960s and serves as a bungalow for officials of the Indian Railways visiting the region. The trains rush past the original platform which is now fenced off, and the last of the sixteen tunnels on the NMR is located nearby.

The Indian Express dated November 19, 1982 reported, "Train services between Mettupalayam and Coonoor will be suspended for two months from Nov. 25 in view of the adverse weather conditions. A press release issued by the Palghat railway division said train service from Coonoor to Udhagamandalam will be operated as usual."

A news report in The Hindu on March 31, 1983 stated, "The Mettupalayam - Ooty train services would be reorganized to provide a fast service to connect the Nilgiri Express."

## Package Tours on NMR

The Times of India, Bombay, reported on April 17, 1983, "As part of the drive of the Indian Railways to develop tourist traffic, the Southern Railway is coming out with an attractive package plan that enables an ordinary middle-class citizen from Madras, Madurai, Ernakulam or Trivandrum to spend two beautiful days in the Nilgiris with not a care regarding accommodation, travel facility for sight-seeing, and the return journey home. The package deal is meant to develop internal tourism and make the picturesque and unique, but uneconomical 46 km mountain railway between Mettupalayam and Ootacamund a growing proposition, if not a profitable one. The Railway looks on this as a social obligation, for the line, laid some three-quarters of a century ago- has only one parallel in the world – in distant Switzerland."

## Railway Board Assurance

The Hindu dated June 14, 1983 reported that the Railway Board chairman, K.T.V. Raghavan, said that "a policy decision had been taken not to close down any uneconomic rail lines, and the Board was thinking of ways to make them viable."

On April 26, 1984, the General Manager of Southern Railway, Arjun Prasad, said that the railway ministry was considering a proposal to "dieselise" the Nilgiri Mountain Railway. He told newsmen that there was no proposal to dismantle and close down the NMR though it was uneconomical. He could not, however, say whether the proposal had been dropped once and for all by the railway ministry.

This was reiterated on May 24, 1985 at Coonoor, by R.K. Jain, the next General Manager of Southern Railway, who said that the feasibility of dieselisation of the trains operating on the Nilgiris ghat section with coal power now was under consideration.

Travel writer, Bill Aitken, in his article "The changing face of Ooty," published in The Statesman, New Delhi on Dec 21, 1985, wrote:

"The rail journey up from Mettupalayam, though not the speediest, remains one of the great steam experiences still left in the world." Bill Aitken also wrote, "The jet age may go and the superjet age may come but some things just don't change. And just as well. Wheezing up the Nilgiri gradient to Ooty is this old Swiss steam locomotive pushing a trainload of vacationers from the back. One of these locos appeared in the film 'A Passage to India', and some are older than Foster's book published in 1924."

An excerpt from a report in The Hindustan Times,
New Delhi dated February 5, 1986:

### New Diesel Engines to Haul Trains to Ooty

"The Southern Railway proposes to induct diesel locomotives on the Mettupalayam-Udhagamandalam (Ooty) metre gauge section, better known as the Nilgiri Railways, which is a major tourist attraction in South India.

According to Mr. K. Vishwanath, General Manager of the Southern Railway the Research Design and Standards Organisation (RDSO) at Lucknow were designing a locomotive suitable for this particular stretch, which climbed from a few hundred feet above mean sea level at Mettupalayam to nearly 7500 feet at Ooty. He said that the locos would have to be of a special type, with attachments called the rack and pinion system, which are also fitted into the rails so that trains could negotiate the steep climb. This sort of arrangement was provided on only one mountain railway in the country – the Nilgiri Railway, as the gradient was one in 12.50, signifying that the height increased by one foot for every 12.50 feet of horizontal movement. In comparison, the Darjeeling Himalayan Railway had a more comfortable gradient of one in 25. The 50-year-old steam locos hauling the trains contributed a great deal to the overall losses, and hence the proposal to replace them by the diesel engines."

To my query, the RDSO, Lucknow in their reply dated 24 October 1986, wrote that the latest information regarding diesel locomotives can be obtained from the Secretary (Traction), Railway Board. On 2 April 1987, the Addl. Executive Director/Traction (Railway Board) S. Ramanathan, wrote that "four of the nine steam locos operating on this section were imported in the early 1950s, and that spares were available from indigenous source. Proposals for introduction of diesel locos on the Nilagiri Railway are under examination by the Railways. There is no likelihood of introducing diesels on this section in the immediate future."

## Stressed Out Vintage Steam Engines on NMR

Meanwhile, the solitary train from Mettupalayam to Ooty suffered heavy delays en route owing to breakdown of the steam engine, necessitating a spare steam engine from Coonoor to be sent down the ghats to rescue the train. So, on rare occasions, one could see the train entering Coonoor several hours behind time, with an engine at both ends of the train, or more hazardously, with an engine attached to the front end instead of its usual position at the rear; the train being pulled uphill by the relief engine sent to rescue the train, and the original engine attached at the rear of the train having been left behind at a wayside station.

## Phasing Out of Steam Engines on Indian Railways

The Times of India, New Delhi dated August 13, 1989 reported "The steam engines are being phased out by 1995 instead of 1998. Once the pride of the Indian Railways, these locos which have gone through a lot of spit and polish may be seen in future only on routes leading to hill stations like Ooty and Darjeeling."

## Television Programme on NMR

On July 17, 1990 the Indian TV channel, Doordarshan, telecast an unannounced programme on the Nilgiri Mountain Railway, which prompted the media critic, Amita Malik, to write:

"Ashok Raina's little vignette on the toy train which goes to Ooty brought unalloyed joy to at least one viewer, as it must have to several more. Trains bring out the childhood wonder in all of us, and the now virtually doomed hill railways are among the few romantic trains left in India. Surely they should be preserved, no matter whether we have moved out of the steam age or not, for children yet to come to enjoy them as much as we did?"

On September 24, 1990 as the Nilagiri Passenger wound its way toward Coonoor from Kallar, it encountered a herd of nearly forty wild elephants, and a calf darted across the track to get hit and killed by the slow moving train. The bereaved pachyderms blocked further progress of the train and menacingly advanced toward it, forcing the crew to pull the train back to Mettupalayam, from where the stranded passengers were sent by road.

## An Unusual Experience

On April 12, 1991, as the passenger train was on its way from Ooty to Mettupalayam, the passengers had an unusual experience when a carriage de-coupled from the rest of the train at Hillgrove. All attempts to re-couple failed and the passengers had to trek down a jungle path to the highway below. Buses were arranged from the state owned Cheran Transport Corporation to take them to Mettupalayam in time to catch the Nilagiri Express bound for Madras Central.

Vikram Sundarji in his article on this railway, 'Over the hill', published in The Times of India, New Delhi on September 21, 1991 wrote, "I walked out somewhat deflated, after having just experienced what must rate as one of the world's most scintillating and original train journeys. I got the feeling that the little toy train's days were numbered."

V. Gangadhar in his article 'Down the memory rails' published in The Hindu, Madras on August 9, 1992 wrote, "Some of the trains had a special attraction for me. The Blue Mountain Express which ran from Madras Central to Ootacamund had its own kind of mystery, taking you to the tall blue hills of Ooty. It was always a pleasure to leave the parched plains of Tamil Nadu."

## Man – Animal Conflict

On March 16, 1993, the train to Ooty which left Mettupalayam at 7.30 A.M. was approaching Adderley station; the passengers noticed a herd of wild elephants strolling nearby. When the train stopped at the station to fill water in the steam locomotive, the crew noticed that the pipeline to the water tank was badly damaged by the thirsty elephants, spoiling all chances of refilling the locomotive's tanks. With no alternative source for filling water, for the uphill journey, the train was reversed back to the base station at Kallar, from where the railway authorities arranged buses to ferry the stranded passengers to Coonoor and Ootacamund, after a further delay of a couple of hours.

## Trial Run of YDM-4 Diesel Loco from Coonoor to Ooty

Also on March 16, 1993, a trial run was conducted with a reconditioned YDM-4 type diesel locomotive (No. 6279) which was brought from Tiruchirapally for use only on the non-rack section from Coonoor to Ootacamund, on the mountain railway. This loco was transported carefully up the ghats to Coonoor, sandwiched between two carriages manned by brakes-men and pushed by a steam engine, at a snail's pace. This is because the diesel locomotive does not have the mechanism to operate on the steep rack and pinion section of the railway.

## Postage Stamps Issued on Mountain Locomotives

To commemorate the hill sections of Indian Railways, The Department of Posts, issued on April 16, 1993, a set of four postage stamps on "Mountain Locomotives," in the following denominations - a Re.1 stamp on the Neral - Matheran Railway, Rs. 6 stamp stamp on the Darjeeling Himalayan Railway, Rs. 8 stamp on the Nilgiri Mountain Railway, and Rs. 11 stamp on the Kalka - Shimla Railway.

## Diesel Traction Between Coonoor and Udhagamandalam

On April 23, 1993, the Southern Railway inaugurated the YDM-4 diesel locomotive, by using it to run the train which came in from Mettupalayam, on the 19-km route between Coonoor and Ooty. Hence the *"specially designed locos"* from RDSO (reported in Feb. 1986) for use on the entire route, were never made, and steam locos continued to run on the rack and pinion section. The train was attached to this diesel loco at Coonoor for its onward trip to Ooty, but the time taken for the journey remained at over five hours, as the steam hauled train from Mettupalayam invariably ran behind time.

## Major Landslide Following Cloudburst Creates a Chasm

On November 11, 1993, following a cloudburst, a major landslip occurred near Runneymede, and half a kilometer of the rail track and over a kilometer of the highway were wiped out along with a few settlements and vehicles, causing some loss of life including that of a wild elephant. The wide chasm created cut off all access by road and rail to between the plains of Coimbatore district and the towns of the Nilgiris district for several days. Several other smaller landslides blocked the rail track at many places on the route.

Nilgiris MP (Member of Parliament) R. Prabhu, has requested Southern Railway to immediately restore the Nilgiris mountain railway track which was damaged in the recent disastrous landslide, reported Indian Express on Dec. 14, 1993. The MP wrote to the Railway Minister,

C.K. Jaffer Sharief that "only half a km of rail track had been damaged as against 1.5 km of the ghat road. He alleged that the Railways had not even assessed the damage to the track so far and the technical committee had not yet visited the site. Even the Railways Divisional Manager (Palakkad) visited the site only on Nov. 30, which was 19 days after the disaster."

Accordingly, track reconstruction work commenced on a war footing by Railway engineers from mid January 1994, and the train services were resumed from March 9, 1994, shortly after the highway was opened after emergency repairs by the Army personnel stationed at Wellington, by rebuilding a kilometer of the roadway and erecting two Bailey bridges as a temporary measure to span the yawning gaps. Concrete bridges have now replaced the temporary Bailey bridges.

The rail track repair took more time as a new path had to be carved out of the hillside to lay a new track over half a kilometer, and sandbags were piled up alongside supported with iron beams driven into the earth to hold the temporary wall, to prevent any further mudslides. These were replaced with a granite revetment after the terrain stabilized. New girders were also installed to erect two new bridges to span the gaps created by the landslide, and to create a channel for the flow of water. Fortunately, a railway tunnel on one side of the chasm was intact and the former alignment of the track was followed to lay a new one. Massive plantation of shrubs and trees was done to prevent further slips, and these took a few years to strike deep roots. Train service was resumed from March 9, 1994 with personnel positioned at the site, holding flags, to guide the train through the spot breached by the landslide. The place now presents a pretty picture with lush greenery all around, and the memory of the landslide has been obliterated forever.

In this context, the landslip, which had wiped out the highway and the railway, creating a large scar of about two kilometers long (when viewed from the air), was partly a man-made disaster. The crown of the hill which had a dense growth of forests was shaved off to plant tea gardens, and to build a tea factory for the newly formed TANTEA (Tamil Nadu Tea) Company, with a view to provide employment for the Tamils from Ceylon (now known as Sri Lanka), who were relocated in the Nilgiris following the Sirimavo Bandaranaike-Lal Bahadur Shastri pact. Another hill near Wellington was also similarly denuded to locate their homes, and the exposed earth of the tea gardens soaked by the unusually heavy rains at that time did the rest of the job!

## Railway Budget – 1995

Meanwhile, in the Railway Budget of March 1995, it was stipulated: "Normal fares for passengers within the Kalka - Shimla, Siliguri - Darjeeling, Mettupalayam - Udagamandalam and Pathankot - Jogindernagar sections. But passengers booked from outside to stations on these sections and vice-versa will continue to pay on the inflated distance basis." On the NMR, the actual distance is 46 km and the chargeable distance is 116 km. - this information used to be printed in the earlier issues of the Southern Railway time-tables, but has been discontinued from the early 1990s.

The Statesman, New Delhi dated May 13, 1995 reported, "There are 31 steam locos left on the narrow gauge section of the Railways. It has been decided that the narrow gauge steam traction on the Darjeeling and Ooty sections will be kept till at least the end of the century as a concession to the 'nostalgia' and also 'engineering marvel, tourism and cultural attraction', according to an official press release. The final decision on its continuation would be taken at the end of that period."

## Centenary Celebration Committee of Coonoor Railway Station Formed

Early in 1997, a Centenary Celebration Committee was formed, comprising prominent rail lovers in Coonoor, with Dr. G.V.J.A. Harshavardhan of the

Vaccine Institute as Convener, to celebrate the centenary of the Coonoor Railway Station which was built in 1897. The embossed insignia on this imposing granite building, NR 1897 (Nilagiri Railway 1897), is visible on the building at the entrance. In the words of Dr. Harshavardhan, "We want to leave an indelible mark of the centenary. We want to open a Railway museum, bring out a souvenir, erect an arch, hold competitions for students and tourists, improve the look of the railway stations, and increase the flow of traffic." Dr. Harshavardhan also said, "We would soon approach the railway authorities with a blue-print for a centenary museum to be run by a registered society."

## Heritage Steam Chariot Inaugurated

The Heritage Steam Chariot, a train leased out to a private agency in the Nilgiri Hills by the Southern Railway, was inaugurated on February 23, 1997, at Udagamandalam, by the Nilgiris District Janta Dal president, N. Chikaiah. The train comprises one 'maharaja' coach and three 'ordinary' coaches, and is hauled by a steam engine. The object of running this train is to encourage tourism as the natural splendour in the Udagamandalam - Runneymede route is enchanting, railway sources said. It also serves to earn some revenue for the NMR. The fare for the round trip journey is Rs. 500 in the maharaja coach and Rs. 250 in the remaining coaches; with piped music, packaged food and beverage, and horse riding included.

A report by K.R. Sreenivas in The Indian Express, New Delhi, March 7, 1997:

## Swiss Steam to Drive Nilgiri Trains

Chennai, March 6: Nearly 98 years ago, the first steam locomotive had chugged along, hauling a set of vintage coaches on the rack rail system of the

Nilgiri Mountain Railway (NMR), one of the most picturesque legacies that the British had left behind. Recent reports that the Railways had decided to do away with the steam engines – and with that the heritage, had hurt many who had taken pride in describing the journeys on the hilly track.

Now comes the news that the Railways are considering placing orders to purchase steam locomotives which will run in the hilly region with assistance from the Swiss government. The Railways propose to purchase four metre gauge rack and adhesion steam locomotives (oil-fired) HG 4/5 for the NMR. These steam locomotives will have a higher hauling capacity to facilitate drawing of more coaches. The tenders for purchasing the steam engines have been cleared by the Railway Board and negotiations are set to commence shortly with the Swiss Locomotive & Machine Works (SLM). The Swiss government has offered a 40 per cent grant and a 60 per cent soft loan to the Indian Railways to procure the steam locomotives for running on the NMR. The SLM has promised a delivery schedule of two to two-and-a-half years once the Indian Railways place the orders.

The decision to purchase new locomotives was taken after a study by De-Consult, a renowned German consultant who went into the feasibility of maintaining the hilly railway.

### A report by G.V. Krishnan in The Sunday Times of India, New Delhi, March 23, 1997:

## They Seek to Keep Coonoor on Tracks

Chennai: A group of railway enthusiasts at Coonoor plan to celebrate the centenary of the Coonoor railway station in a big way.

Established in 1897, the Coonoor railway station was the earliest railhead on the 46-km Nilgiri Mountain Railway (NMR) that connects

Mettupalayam on the foothills with the hill resort of Ooty. Initially, it had 12 railway stations, four of which were closed down in 1962. Regular freight traffic on the NMR was stopped in the early eighties.

The NMR, which was one the prime mode of transport for shipment of tea from the Nilgiris and the sole freight carrier to the hill region, has not been doing well for the past several years. The railway authorities have cut back daily train services between Mettupalayam and Ooty from three to one because of inadequate passenger traffic.

The decline in passenger traffic is attributed to the frequent late arrival of connecting trains at Coimbatore and Mettupalayam. The failure of the Railways to replace old steam engines of 1952 vintage which are prone to breakdowns is cited as the cause of the NMR's unreliability.

"Viewed in this context, the local initiative for the centenary celebrations may well be seen as an attempt by railway enthusiasts to build up public opinion to save the NMR from possible extinction."

## Black Beauty Contest on Nilgiri Mountain Railway

Under the aegis of the Centenary Celebration Committee, the Railway authorities from the Palghat Division of Southern Railway, and those at the Railway Headquarters at Madras (now Chennai) were invited to organise a Black Beauty contest on the Nilgiri Railway, with a view to give due publicity to this mountain rail line.

On April 20, 1997, a Black Beauty contest was held for the first time in the history of the NMR at Coonoor station, featuring three of the oldest steam engines in use, which were judged by a panel of jury from the public (my mother was one of them), on their noise, elegance and mobility. The contest was organised by senior officials of Southern Railway,

Palghat Division, S. Dasarathy and G. Hariradhakrishnan, alongwith the Convener, Centenary Celebration Committee of Coonoor Railway Station, Dr. G.V.J.A. Harshavardhan. A steam engine no. X-37384 which entered service on April 10, 1920, with a failure rate of 1.12 per year was adjudged the 'Queen'.

The Chief Mechanical Engineer, Dasarathy, said three locomotives had been improved functionally to cater to the summer rush of visitors to Ooty, and said that due to inadequate number of engines the running of trains was affected. L.B. Sinha, member, Railway Board, stressed the need for replacing the existing locomotives and said that orders to purchase four oil-fired steam locomotives from Switzerland were being placed.

Dr. Harshavardhan's letter dated April 30, 1997 states, "We met senior railway officials of Railway Board and Southern Railway during their visit to Coonoor on 18, 19 April '97 and were able to make personal representation. Our Committee felt that there is a likelihood of new steam locomotives being inducted into NMR within the next two years. In spite of a general reluctance and inhibition of the Railways to accept proposals from the general public, we now feel that we were able to convince the officials, to some extent, about the urgent need to improve the NMR. We are likely to have a NMR Museum at Coonoor Railway Station for the purpose of preserving its rich heritage. We are of the opinion that the NMR should be operated to satisfy those passengers who are admirers of nature. Privatisation of the line might help, but I am not too sure."

### Train Stranded on the Ghats Near Adderley

Meanwhile, a 'Summer Special' train from Udagamandalam to Mettupalayam, on June 4, 1997, developed a technical snag and halted en route near Adderley station on the rack section of the railway, leaving more than 200 passengers stranded.

Those in the stranded train had to trek about two kilometers through the dense forest, with their luggage, to reach the roadway below, and find accommodation in passing vehicles going toward Mettupalayam.

Due to this, the scheduled Ooty - Mettupalayam passenger train was operated only up to Coonoor from where the passengers were sent by buses to Mettupalayam, to enable them to connect the Nilagiri Express to Chennai.

### "Closure of NMR" Rears Its Head Again?

On August 20, 1997, The Indian Express reported, "The Railway Board in New Delhi is seriously considering the proposal to close down the mountain railway services between Udhagamandalam and Mettupalayam shortly. While confirming the proposal, sources in the Southern Railway said the reason for closing the ghat section was the Railway Ministry's inability to pump in additional funds (around Rs. 100 crore) to purchase at least five locomotive engines as the existing steam engines were outdated, and they could not be used further. Satpal Maharaj, the then Deputy Minister for Railways, had assured that new locomotive engines would be imported at a cost of Rs. 20 crore. But ever since he lost the Railways portfolio, there is no talk about it." The news report also said, "While reeling under severe financial stringency, the railways is not going to go for new engines."

### Trains Suspended Due to Inclement Weather

Trains on the NMR were suspended between Coonoor and Mettupalayam from October 25, 1997 despite there being no landslips, but as a "precautionary measure" according to railway sources, due to the rainy season.

A month later, following heavy rain, landslides occurred and blocked the track. There being no train service, press reporters came to know of it a bit late and they trekked through the forest to reach the spot, and spur the railway personnel into action. "It is actually this attitude of the Railways which is forcing the public to feel that the department is not all that serious in maintaining the service," said P.S. Sundar, a prominent journalist and a strong supporter of this lifeline to Nilgiri Hills.

Commenting on the deteriorating state of affairs on the Nilgiri Railway, U. Sripathi Rao, a long-time-resident of Ooty wrote, "There has been total lack of interest on the part of Indian Railways which has inherited this priceless jewel," and appealed to the Minister for Railways not to allow the Nilgiri Mountain Railway to die an ignominious death. Rao also wrote, "I feel very sad to find we in India have such wonderful things. But we don't enrich our life by improving what we have with us. It is absolutely necessary to improve the Nilgiri Mountain Railway otherwise it will soon have a natural death." (IE, Sep. 9 & Nov. 4, 1997)

### The Indian Express, Coimbatore on November 4, 1997 reported:

### Plea to Restart Train Service

Coonoor: Dr. Harshavardhan, Convener, Centenary Committee of the Coonoor railway station, has urged the Nilgiris Mountain Railway (NMR) to restart its train service, which was stopped a few months ago.

In a statement he regretted the Railway's decision to cancel the train and demanded to introduce more trains between Ooty and Mettupalayam and Ooty and Coonoor. He also suggested that the public should be encouraged to travel by trains.

## Centenary of Coonoor Railway Station (Built in 1897)

The Coonoor Railway Station completed 100 years of existence on December 18, 1997. A Centenary Arch was erected by the Centenary Celebration Committee in the presence of senior railway officials invited by the Committee, at Coonoor station. A postage stamp was to be issued to mark the occasion, but it never materialised. The General Manager, Southern Railway, N. Krithivasan, was grilled by the pressmen who wanted to know why the train service was stopped since October 25th. He replied that "setting right the rail track was a mountainous task and it would take at least three months to restore services on the line." Finally, after nearly three months of closure the train service was restored from January 20, 1998, between Mettupalayam and Ooty.

At the function to erect the imposing and permanent Centenary Arch at the entrance to the Coonoor railway station, noted journalist P.S. Sundar – who has written the largest number of articles on the Nilgiri Mountain Railway (NMR) spanning a period of 34 years, always fighting for the survival, progress, comfort, and safety relating to this train service – was praised by the top brass of Southern Railway for his continuous struggle, and the publicity given which ensured that the NMR was not scrapped. He humbly countered, "The NMR actually ran mostly on newspaper columns than on rails!"

The Indian Express of September 20, 1997 reported, "Dispelling all doubts about the future of the century-old Nilgiris Mountain Railway (NMR) Union Minister of State for Personnel and Parliamentary Affairs, S.R. Balasubramaniam, said here today that it would not be dismantled." He quoted the Railway Minister Ram Vilas Paswan's statement that the NMR would continue its operation in the Hill station. He said that Paswan was keen on importing new locomotives to replace the worn out ones, but admitted that he had not given him any written assurance in this regard.

A Staff Reporter with The Hindu reported on March 29, 1998, "The mountain train on the Nilgiris Mountain Railway (NMR) line between Udhagamandalam and Mettupalayam, which has for several decades been one of the most popular tourist attractions in South India, will continue to chug along with the Southern Railway having taken "effective" steps to improve services on the line.

Having announced that plans were on the anvil to start additional services, a new diesel engine, from the Golden Rock Workshop of the Southern Railway at Tiruchi, was brought to the Nilgiris and pressed into service on the Coonoor – Udhagamandalam section."

### The Indian Express dated March 28, 1998 reported:

### New Diesel Engine in Ooty

Udhagamandalam: The Southern Railway (SR) has brought a new diesel engine (YDM-4 No 6157) here from Tiruchi to operate additional trips between Udhagamandalam and Coonoor. Hari Radhakrishnan, Senior Divisional Manager, Palakkad, was present here when the new engine arrived. By introducing one more diesel engine, the SR has put to rest the speculation that the Nilgiris Mountain Railway is going to be closed.

Meanwhile, heavy rain and landslides forced the suspension of trains from Dec. 1, 1998, on the ghat section between Coonoor and Mettupalayam, till further notice.

The Hindu of December 11, 1998 reported, "Train services on the Nilgiris Mountain Railway (NMR) line between Coonoor and

Mettupalayam, which were suspended around the beginning of this month, following sections of the track being affected by landslides near Adderley have not yet been restored. Meanwhile more slips have reportedly occurred in some places."

## The Indian Express dated December 24, 1998 reported:

### Railway Stations Closed

Railway stations at Lovedale, Ketti, Aravankadu and Wellington have remained closed for the past several days. As the above stations are located between Udhagamandalam and Coonoor, trains on the ghat sections have been cancelled. The employees in these stations were sent to stations outside the district. However, Coonoor and Udhagamandalam stations are functioning. The closure has raised doubts as to whether the Southern Railway plans to permanently close the stations due to heavy loss. However, sources said the closure was temporary as the ghat section track was in the process of being cleared. The work is on at a fast pace.

## The Hindu of Tuesday, December 29, 1998 reported:

While it is an established fact that a visit to the Nilgiris is not complete without a ride on the unique Nilgiris Mountain Railway (NMR) line between Udhagamandalam and Mettupalayam, the delay in resuming services on that line, which was affected by landslides in the recent rains, is causing concern to the people here. However Railway sources told this Correspondent that the track between Udhagamandalam and Coonoor had been cleared and the closed stations would be reopened, and the affected area between Coonoor and Mettupalayam would be set right shortly.

The television channel, SUN TV, reported on January 15, 1999, that train services on the NMR were resumed from that day, after a period of a month and a half of closure.

**Excerpts from a report by S. Gururajan in**
**The New Indian Express dated January 18, 1999:**

### NMR Struggling for Survival, Thanks to Government Apathy

Coimbatore, Jan 17: A proposal to get new engines for the 100-year-old Nilgiri Mountain Railway (NMR) has been shelved thanks to the lethargy of the Central Government. The proposal to revive and rejuvenate the train service has been conveniently forgotten as the Ministries of Railway and Finance are at loggerheads over financial matters.

Speaking to *The New Indian Express*, Dr. Harshavardhan, Secretary of the Nilgiri Mountain Railway Society, which has been fighting for the cause of the oldest railway system, said that NMR had managed to survive despite many ups and downs in the past ten years or so.

Whenever the NMR was threatened with imminent closure, promises would be made for its revival only to be forgotten later. Representations were made to the Central Government, top Southern Railway officials like General Manager at Chennai and the Divisional Railway Manager of Palakkad division in the past two years regarding the plight of NMR, but in vain.

The Palakkad based Southern Railway Employees Sangh (SRES) also submitted a detailed petition explaining the condition of the employees working and appealed to save the NMR from certain death.

Dr. Harshavardhan said whenever the issue was raised with top railway officials they offered mere lip service and did nothing thereafter. He had met the Chairman of the Railway Board also in New Delhi, to help improve the lot of this mountain railway.

## Proposal to Buy New Engines from SLM Abandoned?

Even though none in the capital understood the significance of the NMR, the Railway Board evinced some interest in granting a new lease of life to it. After repeated attempts, it was proposed (in 1997) to purchase four engines from the original manufacturers, Schweizerische Lokomotiv und Maschinenfabrik (SLM), Winterthur, Switzerland. After prolonged negotiations, the company offered to fabricate one engine at a subsidised price of Rs. 12 crore, and suggested that the remaining three engines could be imported in knocked down condition and assembled in India, as this would further lower the price to Rs. 8 crore. However, nothing more has been heard regarding the purchase of the engines for the past two years. An appeal was made to the Union Government to bring out a postal stamp to commemorate the upcoming centenary of the prestigious railway line in the country but the appeal seemed to have fallen on the deaf ears of the bureaucracy.

## Clamour to Link Coonoor & Ootacamund to PRS

On February 2, 1999, a letter was sent to the Chairman, Railway Board, Ministry of Railways, New Delhi, to apprise the Ministry of the urgency to have the vintage locomotives in use on the NMR replaced by importing new ones, since no locomotive manufacturing company of the Railways in India has been able to build one suitable for the special track of the NMR, despite the expertise available.

It was also mentioned that though linked by railway, Udhagamandalam and Coonoor are not linked by the Railways' PRS (Passenger Reservation

System, or computerised reservations and ticketing) facility, but, in the Northern Railway even the out-agencies like Mussoorie – which has no railway, and Shimla, on the Kalka - Shimla Railway were linked.

No reply was received though the letter was sent by registered mail, thereby showing the sorry state of our government departments. Another letter sent later, to the English daily 'The New Indian Express', was published in their issue of March 2, 1999. This letter specifies, "Though linked by the railway network, Coonoor and Ooty lack the computerised ticket reservation facility. People from the Nilgiris have to go to Mettupalayam or Coimbatore to reserve tickets. Hence computerised reservations must be introduced at Coonoor, Udagamandalam and the Out-agency at Kotagiri."

## Southern Railway Attempts to Convert Steam Engine to Oil Firing

A vintage engine X-37390 was sent to Tiruchy for conversion to oil firing at the Golden Rock Works in 1997, and brought to Coonoor after the modifications. However it being the first attempt to convert the engine, the trial runs were not satisfactory and trials were cancelled. The locomotive remained idle on a siding at Coonoor for almost a year, till it was later withdrawn from active service, and the oil firing mechanism was removed to restore the engine's original look.

## Vignette on National Rail Museum

The Times of India, New Delhi, had the following vignette on the National Rail Museum at New Delhi, "Have you ever seen a double-decker passenger coach in India? Or wondered why trains climbing uphill don't roll back? Or why the Nilgiri Railway system in India ranks among the finest in the world? At the Indoor Gallery, you will find answers to all this and more, besides getting an insight to the railways' present and future projects."

# N.M.R. – 100 Years and After

## Nilgiri Mountain Railway Centenary – June 15, 1999

The Nilgiri Mountain Railway, opened on June 15, 1899, having completed 100 years of service to the nation, a special function was held at Coonoor, in the presence of an august gathering (which included this author), to celebrate the Centenary. The function, on June 15, 1999, was attended by the Union Minister for Railways, Nitish Kumar, who was the Chief Guest. He arrived at Coonoor on a "Inspection Special" train from Mettupalayam, along with other senior officials of Southern Railway. A military band, from the Madras Regimental Center at Wellington, welcomed the Minister on arrival at Coonoor.

The General Manager, Southern Railway, Krithivasan, who welcomed the gathering said, "The age-old steam locos with unique rack cylinders were being maintained with the expertise available with SR. A global tender for replacement of these locomotives was called some time back but the high cost quoted did not allow for further progress; and now another global tender has been floated."

While seated on the specially erected platform along with other dignitaries, the Railway Minister had in his speech promised to link Coonoor and Udagamandalam with the PRS (Passenger Reservation System), and that this railway would be modernised and electrified for efficient and speedy travel. He announced, "NMR would be an ultramodern railway." He also stressed, "Though the operations are not economically viable, the railways will spare no efforts to keep the system working, taking into account the antique and heritage value of the system, and also the interest of tourists. We have to maintain this at any cost." A preliminary survey was to commence on the following week, to electrify the Coimbatore – Mettupalayam - Udagamandalam route. The outcome of the survey has not been made known, perhaps meeting the same fate as all ministerial promises.

## The First Mounted Display of Steam Engine on NMR Unveiled

On the occasion of the Centenary of Nilgiri Mountain Railway, the vintage Swiss-built steam engine X-37390 was unveiled on its mount outside Coonoor railway station by Railway Minister, Nitish Kumar. This steam engine was built in 1922 by SLM at Winterthur and had logged 7.5 lakh km in its 75 years of service from Oct 1923, as per the engraved stone plaque erected alongside.

## Special Postal Cover and Cancellation for NMR Centenary

The Department of Posts had promised to release a stamp on the occasion of the NMR Centenary year, but it turned out to be just a special cancellation with a postal cover issued on the occasion by S. Jayaraman, the Chief Post Master General, Tamilnadu Circle.

A request to the authorities at New Delhi to have a stamp issued was sent on October 31, 1996, well in advance of the event on June 15, 1999; mentioning that a stamp was issued to mark the 100 years of the Darjeeling

Himalayan Railway. A reply dated December 12, 1996 was received from the Asst. Director General (Philately), P.D. Tshering, regretting to consider the proposal. He wrote, "A stamp has already been released on Nilgiri Mountain Railway on 16–4–93. As a matter of policy, this Department does not issue more than one stamp on the same issue."

However, when questioned about the *"same issue"* aspect, and, how two stamps were issued on Darjeeling Railway (one for the DHR Centenary – in 1982, and another among the Mountain Locomotives- on April 16, 1993), besides innumerable stamps on Mahatma Gandhi and others, no response was received from the Department of Posts as they were clearly stumped!

In the latest instance, despite having a stamp on a steam engine of the Kalka – Shimla railway released on April 16, 1993, in the set of stamps on Mountain Locomotives, this railway was again honoured with a stamp on completing 100 years of service on Nov. 9, 2003. Clearly, NMR is given a step-motherly treatment by the Ministry of Railways, and the Government of India.

## Internal Assessment of Heritage Value

A track inspection ride was conducted on June 24, 1999 on the 20 km rack-section between Coonoor and Kallar, travelling downhill by trolley. The author was accompanied by Dr. G.V.J.A.Harshavardhan, Secretary, NMR Society and Manoharan, Permanent Way Engineer, and the trolley-man Moosa. The party was flagged off at Coonoor by the Station Master, Radhakrishnan. This was part of an internal assessment of the heritage value of the NMR, and to inspect the ongoing track maintenance work at a few points en route. The non-motorised trolley was brought back uphill in a railway wagon, from the base station at Mettupalayam.

## NMR on Discovery Channel "Extreme Machines"

In August 1999, the NMR featured in the Discovery Channel's television documentary "Extreme Machines" showing locomotives and trains – past and present, from all over the world. The special track and a train running between Adderley and Hillgrove were telecast in the programme.

## Reserved Accommodation Sought on NMR Trains

On August 26, 1999, the NMR Society, Coonoor, urged Southern Railway to introduce computerised reservations at Coonoor, and to introduce a reserved compartment on the NMR trains. This suggestion was given by several citizens who wrote to the media, urging the railways to link Coonoor and Ooty to the Passenger Reservation System (PRS). Suitable requests were also made to the Railway Minister, Ms. Mamata Banerjee by the politicians from Tamilnadu.

## 'Nilgiris By Night' Tourist Train

"Nilgiris by night," a tourism related rail project promoted by the Indian Railway Catering and Tourism Corporation (IRCTC) and a private agency, Ashirwad Heritage Tours, was inaugurated at the Ooty station by the Nilgiris District Collector, Ms. Supriya Sahu, on January 5, 2002. Commencing the journey at 10 P.M. from Ooty, the train reached Ketti via Lovedale. At Ketti, the promoters entertained the passengers to dinner. The train then proceeded to Coonoor from where the group, returned to Ooty by road in the wee hours of the morning. Later, another such trip was run exclusively for a few foreigners.

## Bridge No. 55 Destroyed By Landslide

Train services on the Coonoor - Mettupalayam route were cancelled following landslides due to heavy rains from December 25, 2001 onwards, as a bridge (No. 55) was completely destroyed near Hillgrove. A train, which had departed from Mettupalayam for Ooty that morning returned from Kallar due to the breached track. New pillars had to be built and iron girders procured to repair the bridge, all material being transported by rail to the site. The train services were restored from April 1, 2002, after a trial run was conducted a couple of days earlier. The Southern Railway General Manager, V. Anand, who visited the spot to inspect the restoration work on March 19, 2002, said: "A proposal to electrify the Nilgiri Mountain rail track between Mettupalayam and Ooty is under the consideration of the Central Government."

## PRS Facility Opens at Coonoor

On May 11, 2002, in commemoration of "150 years of Indian Railways," the Southern Railway inaugurated a computerised Passenger Reservation System (PRS) centre at Coonoor. On this occasion, a 'Commemorative Steam Run' from Mettupalayam to Coonoor was flagged off by the Union Minister of State for Railways and Parliamentary Affairs, O. Rajagopal. Four months later, on September 21, 2002, a computerised reservation office was opened at Udagamandalam station. The efforts taken by the public of the Nilgiri Hills to have the facility thus bore fruit.

The Passenger Reservation System (PRS) is supposed to enable a traveller to reserve his ticket for a journey from a computerised reservation centre in any part of India to Coonoor or Ooty and vice versa. However, in practice it is not so. When asked for a ticket from Chennai (formerly Madras) to Coonoor, at the Indian Railways booking counter at the Indira Gandhi. International airport in Delhi, the booking clerk could not locate Coonoor on his system, despite providing him with the station code, ONR. After some trials, he could locate Mettupalayam, and so he stated that no ticket could be issued beyond Mettupalayam. A tourist from New Delhi, C. Nandakumar, who visited to Udagamandalam in June 2006, was wise enough to contact a relative at Coimbatore who bought a ticket for the mountain railway train, and handed it over to him while he travelled from Chennai Central to Mettupalayam by the 'superfast' Nilagiri Express which halts for 30 min at Coimbatore en route. This fact was corroborated by the Station Master, Coonoor, G. Saravanan, who claimed that it was a "software problem" and needed rectification. The moot point is that the problem persisted for the past four years, and no attempt was made to rectify this anomaly, and despite the fact that reserved accommodation is available now on the NMR - 16 seats in First Class and 80 seats in Second Class.

## Poor Publicity on NMR

As for the Railways' publicity, if one glances through the pages of the time-tables "Trains at a glance" published annually by Indian Railways, Coonoor and Udagamandalam do not exist, as also the trains scheduled to run on the NMR. The route to Shimla and the 'express trains' thereon are shown in the time table. Due to this, any person who refers to it would conclude that there is no train service to Ooty, and, the countrywide computerised reservation system also does not have Coonoor or Udagamandalam, despite being linked to the PRS (Passenger Reservation System).

The 'Trains at a Glance' time tables are referred to by the personnel manning the Government of India Tourist Information counters at the airports in the gateway cities of India, and so will provide wrong information to any prospective tourist. To verify this point while on the job in Air-India, I accosted the person manning the Tourist Information desk at the Indira Gandhi International Airport, Delhi, inquiring how to reach Udagamandalam by rail. He replied, "There is no train service to Ooty. You can fly to Bangalore and then reach Ooty by road." I then gave him a photocopy of the Nilagiri Railway schedules in force and told him not to misguide prospective tourists with wrong information. He was in fact unaware of the very existence of the NMR, and as I found out later, so did most others in the Capital of India!

The Southern Railway time table, however, has details of trains on the NMR, but "Trains at a glance" time tables are supposed to have them too, but only 'Mail/Express trains' are shown in the latter. For proper information, all slow and fast trains, whether 'Express' or 'Passenger', must figure in the all-India time tables "Trains at a glance". The Railways should amend subsequent issues of the schedules accordingly to be very informative to the vast majority of railway travellers. Statistics reveal that 10 million passengers are transported daily by 11000 trains on the 65000 km network of Indian Railways - the second largest railway network in the world (in 2000).

## Modified Steam Engine on Trial: May 2002

Owing to shortage of high grade coal for the steam engines, the Swiss-built engines began to develop snags and stall en route on the ascent between Kallar and Coonoor, and fears of closure of the line loomed large again. At his stage, there was much public pressure to stall this move and save the railway line. In 1997, Southern Railway had begun experimenting to convert one coal fired engine to run on furnace oil, under the leadership of Mr. Jaisingh, Chief Motive Power Engineer (CMPE/MAS). However, as the trials on this old engine X-37390 were not very satisfactory it was withdrawn from service, and the other remaining Swiss-built steam engines were sent to Golden Rock Workshop at Tiruchirapally for modification to oil-firing using advanced technology.

Accordingly another engine X-37395 was converted and brought to Mettupalayam for trials on the hill section. As per Station Master, Sivasamy, of Mettupalayam station, this steam engine, besides easing problems of procuring coal and cost effectiveness, would also reduce the pressure on manpower. The modification of the vintage engine was at a cost of Rs. 30 lakh. These trials were challenging, and the section engineers namely Harinarayanan and Jayachandran contributed much for its success, said V. Nandakumar, Station Master, Coonoor.

## Oil Fired Steam Engine Successful

On September 22, 2002, the "oil fired steam engine" number X-37395 successfully operated the passenger train from Mettupalayam to Coonoor. It had undergone several trial runs and 35 experts from Bharat Heavy Electricals Ltd., Cummins, Grund Fos, Wesman, Thermax, and engineers from a firm named TREC-STEP, brought about the necessary improvements. The modification was done as importing new oil-fired steam locos (class HG 45) from Switzerland were prohibitively expensive at Rs. 30 crores per locomotive. It may be noted that the Railways had planned (in March 1997) to import four new steam engines from the original manufacturers at Winterthur, Switzerland.

## Poor State of Existing Steam Engines

Owing to the total lack of interest on the part of the Indian Railways which has inherited this priceless jewel, and the deteriorating condition of the vintage steam locos which require to be replaced anew, the time is not far off when this unique piece of engineering skill would pass into oblivion.

As for the YDM-4 diesel locomotives used on the Coonoor to Udagamandalam route of this railway, these were merely brought here from the main line metre gauge network of the railway system. They are not specially made for the NMR and do not have the mechanism for operating on the rack and pinion section. The locomotive is longer than the carriages and present a rather out of place look, unlike the 700 horse power ZDM-3 type locos used on the narrow gauge mountain railways to Shimla and the Kangra valley, which are of the same length as the steam engines used there earlier. The Darjeeling Himalayan Railway has a specially made narrow gauge diesel locomotives (NDM-6) built by the Chittaranjan Locomotive Works, Calcutta, to haul trains from May 21, 2000.

**Tourist Special Train**

The Southern Railway, which introduced chartered trips on the NMR two years ago, conducted their third such trip on June 19, 2004, when 116 employees of a Chennai based private firm travelled on the NMR as part of a company-sponsored holiday. The 'Tourist Special' train was operated from Mettupalayam to Udagamandalam, and the cost of chartering a trip on the NMR was Rs. 19000. Railway sources said that the demand for chartering trips on NMR was increasing and that early next year a trip would be operated for a group of tourists from France.

**Trains Disrupted Again**

Trains on the Mettupalayam - Coonoor were stopped from October 10, 2002 onwards due to several landslips following heavy rainfall. The track was restored after eight days.

On April 20, 2003, one of the coaches of the train to Ooty from Mettupalayam derailed near Kallar station. According to Railway sources,

"This was the first time in history that the mountain train, which runs at a speed of 13 km, has derailed." About 250 passengers who were consequently stranded were transported by buses to the hill station.

On October 27, 2003 trains on the Udagamandalam - Coonoor route were suspended for a day when a wheel of the diesel locomotive (YDM-4) went off the track while hauling a passenger train between Coonoor and Ooty. This was the first incident involving a diesel locomotive on the Nilgiri Mountain Railway, introduced for running trains only on the non-rack route between Coonoor and Ooty. The engine was re-railed and taken back to Coonoor late in the night, and an inquiry was initiated.

# N.M.R. – A World Heritage Site

After much effort since 2002, by steam enthusiasts in India and abroad, and efforts by the people of the Nilgiri Hills, two delegates nominated by the United Nations Educational, Scientific and Cultural Organisation (UNESCO), Robert Lee and Ian Walker, travelled on a "Inspection Special" train from Mettupalayam to Udagamandalam on September 27, 2004; to inspect the track and its working, in order to assess the heritage value.

The delegates inspected the stations en route and the locomotive sheds at Mettupalayam and Coonoor, examining the components and accessories that kept the ancient railway system going. They had to submit their reports to the International Council for Monuments and Sites of UNESCO at Paris. They were accompanied by Sandeep Mehra, Director, National Rail Museum, New Delhi, Rajesh Agrawal, Consultant-Indian Railways for UNESCO, and the Divisional Railway Manager, Palghat (now known as Palakkad) Division, S.K. Sharma.

## NMR Becomes UNESCO's World Heritage Site

On July 15, 2005, the World Heritage Committee of UNESCO had a meeting at Durban, South Africa. N.M.R. was the only entry whose nomination was unanimously supported by all the 20 member countries. Accordingly UNESCO declared the Nilgiri Mountain Railway as a World Heritage site for its outstanding contribution in keeping steam heritage tourism alive. The UNESCO committee said, "NMR is a unique example of construction genius employed by railway engineers in the 19th century. Before the railway, it took over 10 days to reach Ooty, braving insects and wild animals. Now the 46 km. journey takes only four hours. Various facets of the railway line, its rack and pinion mechanism to gain height, the steam engines, coaches, the station buildings preserved in their original shape, all bear testimony to the technological skills of a bygone era. NMR is also the best example of a colonial railway and part of that stage of globalisation, which was characterised by the political and economic domination of the people of Asia, Africa and the Pacific, by Europeans."

The UNESCO inscription is an extension of the earlier nomination of the Darjeeling Himalayan Railway as a heritage site. The Nilgiri Mountain Railway, along with the Darjeeling Himalayan Railway is now part of UNESCO's "Mountain Railways of India."

In the words of travel columnist Bill Aitken, "India becomes the only country to flaunt a second feather in its transport cap by the Nilgiri Mountain Railway being unanimously elected into the select UNESCO list."

A seasoned traveller K.N. Purandar commented, "The most memorable journey I had undertaken was from Mettupalayam to Ooty – a slow, uphill trip which enabled me to observe nature in all its enchanting glory."

## NMR Day at Udagamandalam Station

NMR Day was celebrated on October 15, 2005 to commemorate the date of opening of the Ooty station – it was opened on October 15, 1908. As a special gesture, the oil-fired steam engine no. X-37395 hauled the train to Ooty on that day, instead of the normally used YDM-4 diesel engine. The Collector of the Nilgiris, C. Vijayaraj Kumar, and K. Natarajan, founder of the Heritage Steam Chariot Trust were among those who participated in the celebrations. Davassy (66) who was long associated with the NMR as a trolley-man was a guest. All the stations between Ooty and Coonoor wore a festive look on the occasion. A specially ordered cake was cut and distributed among all visitors and passengers at Ooty station.

## World Heritage Plaques Unveiled

Plaques to mark the dedication of the Nilgiri Mountain Railway as a World Heritage site in July 2005 were unveiled at Coonoor and Ooty stations on November 21, 2005 by the Union Minister of State for Railways, R. Velu, who promised a sum of Rs. 20 lakhs, and said, "The funds would be used for re-laying tracks, building of new coaches and modernisation of railway stations." It is hoped that funds are duly allocated and properly utilised.

The Minister also said, "Indian Railways will continue to run the trains considering that they have been given heritage status, whether they earn profits or suffer losses, and the Indian Railways and India were proud of these systems because of the unique technological success during the 19th century." He also mentioned that NMR incurs an annual loss of Rs. 5 crore.

## Deteriorating State of the World Heritage Railway

Unfortunately, the recognition by UNESCO failed to improve the condition of the NMR, as minor derailments – unheard of before in the history of the now 108-year old railway – marred the scene.

On the morning of August 28, 2005, coaches of a passenger train which arrived from Ooty derailed at Coonoor station while it was being shunted from the platform to an adjacent line, to make way for the Mettupalayam - Ooty Passenger which was nearing Coonoor. Four pairs of wheels of the third coach and one pair of the second derailed. There were totally four coaches. As the track was blocked, the incoming train from Mettupalayam was halted outside the station, and the remaining train services for the day were cancelled.

On January 17, 2006, the wheels of a steam engine of the Nilagiri Passenger chugging along merrily uphill at a speed of about 10 km per hour left the track soon after crossing bridge No. 19 between Kallar and Hillgrove as the clamps in the track broke due to the weight of the train. The stranded passengers, including some foreign tourists, had to board buses for Coonoor and Ooty, after a strenuous descent through forest paths to reach the road.

This derailment caused shockwaves among the people of the Nilgiris, who pointed out that the NMR was a "proud possession" of the Nilgiri Hills, and hoped that top priority would be accorded by the Railway Ministry to ascertain the cause of the derailment.

Though train services resumed the next day, the train from Mettupalayam reached Ooty three hours behind schedule due to engine problem en route.

On January 18, 2006, the engine of a 'Special train' carrying the Chief Mechanical Engineer from Chennai derailed at almost the same spot. The cause of this mishap is yet to be ascertained.

On January 21, 2006, a piston rod of the steam engine pinion mechanism broke while the Nilagiri Passenger with about 200 passengers aboard was negotiating the ghats about three kilometers from Kallar en route to Coonoor. The stranded passengers were forced to trek about four kilometers through unfamiliar mountain paths in the forest and sustained minor bruises. An American tourist, John Smith, said, "It was a great disappointment for us. We had to walk through an unfamiliar forest area.

We have been planning for several months to travel in the heritage train. Unfortunately, we could not enjoy the travel." Another tourist said, "The Railways should give proper attention to the maintenance of this train. It was a disappointment for all, both tourists and local passengers."

On April 30, 2006, the steam engine of a train from Mettupalayam with over 250 aboard, including foreigners, chugging uphill at about 7 km per hour almost derailed, shortly after it began its ascent from Kallar. Buses were arranged to ferry the tourists from Kallar.

Though all these derailments occurred within a short span of each other and without any injury to passengers, as the trains were running at a very slow speed and the driver could stop the train in a jiffy; it does bring to the fore the deteriorating state of the track and the maintenance of the rolling stock.

On June 10, 2006, the Nilagiri Passenger on its way from Mettupalayam got stuck at the outskirts of Coonoor, as the entire stock of coal stored in the engine was used up! Such an incident has never occurred since the inception of this railway. The staff at Coonoor station transported coal by road to the site in the three-wheeled autorickshaws, to rescue the stranded train, which reached after a delay of four hours. As per the Southern Railway sources, the poor quality of coal stocked by them is the reason for this, and said that the problem was likely to continue till the present stock was utilised and fresh stocks arrived. The Railways said they would monitor the quality of coal.

On June 11, 2006, the steam engine failed between Kallar and Adderley stations when pushing a train, ostensibly due to poor quality of coal, leaving the passengers in the lurch once more, making a travel by the NMR an arduous experience as the train never runs on time. "We got into a truck," said Theresa Victor from United Kingdom, who was among a group of foreigners on the train. "While we were disappointed that we could not travel by the NMR, thanks to the failure of the Railways, we had another new experience – travelling through the ghat section in a truck!"

Also due to the solitary train service on the line, and that too with fewer carriages, there is a capacity constraint. More than the comfortable number of passengers board the train, and the carriages are overloaded. Many a time one can see the wheel axles glowing red and smoke emanating from them, due to application of brakes in the overloaded coaches. Tourists who come to these hill stations who plan to travel by the NMR are therefore a disappointed lot, as they are denied accommodation and have to travel by road.

A point to be noted here is that of the five vintage steam engines left on the NMR, only one (numbered X-37395) has been converted to oil firing; and whenever the oil fired locomotive is attached to a train at Mettupalayam, it reaches Coonoor about thirty minutes ahead of the time published in the latest time-table!

## Bio-Diesel Locomotives for Coonoor – Ooty Trains

On July 2–3, 2006, the two YDM-4 diesel locomotives stabled at Coonoor were taken back to the plains, separately, by attaching them in between two passenger coaches manned by brakesmen, and cautiously hauled downhill by a steam engine. Two more YDM-4 diesel locomotives (Nos. 6225 and 6331) painted light green, and running on bio-diesel, a fuel extracted from the seeds of "Jatropha" plants (*Jatropha curcas sp.*) were introduced for operating trains on the Coonoor – Udagamandalam route. G. Saravanan, Station Master, Coonoor said that the new locos were "environment friendly".

## Media Points Out Lapse By Railways

The first anniversary of the Nilgiri Mountain Railway being declared a World Heritage site (July 15, 2006) passed by unnoticed due to the attitude of the Railway authorities. The media pointed out the lapse and hoped that the Southern Railway would make an in-depth study of the NMR, and iron out all shortcomings. Railway enthusiasts lamented that the lack of efforts to maintain the NMR properly is quite apparent, and said, "The attitude of the authorities concerned in allowing the first anniversary of the line being declared a World Heritage site to pass by unnoticed was akin to adding insult to injury."

## Run of Heritage Steam Chariot

On October 2, 2006, to celebrate the birthday of Mahatma Gandhi, a special run of the Heritage Steam Chariot was conducted up to Runneymede, where a function was organised, as it is believed that the ashes of the Mahatma were placed at this station. There is, however, nothing to substantiate this belief historically or otherwise. The founder of the Heritage Steam Chariot Trust, Natarajan, held a function at Ooty station to celebrate NMR Day on October 15, 2006, to mark the 98th anniversary of the opening of the Coonoor - Udagamandalam section of the mountain railway. A cake shaped like a train with a steam engine was cut on the occasion and distributed among those present, and the passengers who arrived by the train from Mettupalayam, which was specially hauled by an oil-fired steam engine between Coonoor and Udagamandalam instead of the usual diesel engine. The Southern Railway authorities were conspicuous by their absence, but, the Collector of Nilgiris, Santosh K. Misra, was present on the occasion.

## NE Monsoon Rains Damage Hillgrove – Kallar Railtrack

Meanwhile, the North East monsoon having set in, the Nilgiris had copious rainfall resulting in the cancellation of the rail service between Coonoor and Mettupalayam from October 18, 2006 due to landslips blocking the route between Kallar and Hillgrove stations on the NMR. Though through traffic was restored in a couple of days, a further spell of heavy showers caused a large boulder to roll down the hillside and block the entrance to tunnel no. 7 on the mountain railway, which was cleared in two days. Subsequent spells of heavy rain caused landslips and the fall of more mud and boulders between Kallar and Hillgrove blocking the rack section of the railway in about six places, causing an indefinite closure of the line, as continuous rain slowed down restoration work. Rail traffic continued to operate between Coonoor and Udagamandalam, as this section of the track was unaffected by landslides.

Even though the 27-km track between Coonoor and Mettupalayam was cleared by November 10, 2006, and trains were run for two days, heavy rainfall – 129 mm in 24 hrs on November 13, 2006 - caused several landslips and buried the track, forcing suspension of train services. The winding track and some tunnels were blocked with rain-soaked mud, rocks, and fallen trees. Owing to continuous heavy rains and lack of easy access, no evaluation of the damage could be carried out immediately.

Extensive damage was also caused to the main highway between Mettupalayam and Coonoor, near Burliar, effectively cutting off all access to the hills from the plains. Floodwaters washed away a bridge, along with sections of the roadway and a loaded lorry groaning its way uphill. The Madras Regimental Centre stationed at Wellington swung into action to erect a temporary Bailey bridge, and heavy machinery was pressed into service by the Highways Department to restore the road link within a month, for light traffic. Heavy vehicular traffic was diverted, from Coonoor, on a longer route via Kotagiri to the plains at Mettupalayam, to avoid further damage to the newly repaired ghat road, now renamed as National Highway 67 stretching from Mysore to Nagapattinam via Ooty and Coimbatore.

## Track Restoration Takes Three Months

The railway route between Kallar and Coonoor, being on a largely inaccessible terrain, posed a major problem as all the equipment and the manpower needed to restore the track had to be sent only by rail. The blocked areas along the line were cleared stage by stage, and a girder was transported to the site of the breached bridge. Over 35000 cubic metres of mud and rocks were removed, and the track was restored for through traffic on January 20, 2007, after three months of closure, at a cost of over Rs. 90 lakh.

## Swiss Television Documentary on NMR

A four-member team from the Swiss National Television visited NMR in March 2007 to make a documentary film on the 110-yr old railway, as it had a Swiss connection. A team member, Marcus Storrer, said that modifications were being tried out on the mountain locomotives in Switzerland in such a manner that their heritage value is not affected.

## Everyone's Wish

As P.S. Sundar, a concerned resident of Coonoor rightly said, "One thing is certain – every one wants the NMR to puff its way safely and on time, every single day through the 45.88 km rails with 20 km of rack and pinion section, crossing 208 curves, 250 bridges and 16 tunnels in a gradient of 1 in 12.50, making this Asia's steepest and longest metre gauge mountain railway unique amidst the unparalleled natural beauty of the Nilgiris."

## Vintage NMR Equipment at National Rail Museum, Delhi

A condemned Swiss steam engine no. X-37385, built in 1918, and a vintage wooden composite carriage (with Ist and IIIrd Class accommodation) used on this railway are stabled at the National Rail Museum in New Delhi, along with a sample of the rack bars. A working model of the rack railway is displayed in the indoor gallery of the museum, to acquaint visitors of this unique traction.

## Try This Simple Quiz

**Consider the following about the Nilgiri Mountain Railway:**

1. It connects Mettupalayam with Udagamandalam.
2. The work on this Railway was started as early as 1895 A.D.
3. M. Riggenbach was the brainchild behind this project.
4. In the year 2005, it has been included in the World Heritage List.

**Out of the above, find the correct set of statements:**

   **a)** 1, 2, and 3   **b)** 2, 3, and 4   **c)** 1, 3 and 4   **d)** 1, 2, 3 and 4

# Odyssey to Oblivion?

As the UNESCO World Heritage Nilgiri Mountain Railway entered its 109th year of service, mechanical problems continued to cause considerable hardship to the travellers.

## Recent Incidents

On May 10, 2007, passengers who boarded the "Summer Special" train from Mettupalayam at 9 A.M had an unforgettable experience. The steam engine lost its pushing power as it ascended the hills, stopping almost sixteen times between Kallar and Hillgrove. At Hillgrove, it was stopped longer till a relief train from Coonoor reached with 40 bags of coal. Using this coal, the stranded train finally reached Coonoor shortly after 6 P.M instead of the scheduled 1.20 P.M and travellers aboard were highly inconvenienced.

On May 27, 2007, boulders and mudslides following rains damaged 60 metres of the rail track on the ghats, causing a damage to the une of Rs. 40 lakh. A band of 150 workers worked round-the-clock to restore it in five days.

On June 4, 2007 the engine of the Nilagiri Passenger from Mettupalayam developed a mechanical snag near Kallar. A spare engine (meant for the "Summer Special" which was to follow it) was dispatched to rescue the train which proceeded onwards toward Ooty. Thereby the "special" train remained cancelled.

On June 8, 2007, the steam engine of the train from Mettupalayam to Udagamandalam developed a fault near Hillgrove, as it was negotiating a tunnel. A relief engine was dispatched from Coonoor, and the stranded train was brought to Coonoor several hours late. As a result, the corresponding service to Mettupalayam was cancelled.

All these incidents of mechanical snags in the few steam engines left on the NMR, and the poor quality of coal stocked by the Railways is a matter of grave concern as to the future of this UNESCO World Heritage Site – the Nilgiri Mountain Railway.

## Second Engine Converted from Coal to Oil Firing

Meanwhile, like a *light at the end of a tunnel*, it was reported in the newspapers that the Railways workshop at Golden Rock, Tiruchirappally, was in the process of converting four of the vintage steam engines to run on furnace oil instead of coal, at a cost of Rs. 40 crore. Two of these converted engines were brought to the Coonoor loco shed and underwent extensive trials. One of these 1952-vintage engines, X-37391, was seen to be successfully hauling passenger trains on the ghat section in October 2007. "One more oil-fired steam engine would be commissioned after trials," said G. Saravanan, Station Master, Coonoor, shortly before his transfer to Coimbatore North station. With these in action, three old engines converted to oil firing will be in operation on this line.

## New Light-Weight Carriages Arrive

In September 2007, four revamped carriages were flagged off for use on the NMR, at the Golden Rock workshop, by V. Carmelus, the Chief

Mechanical Engineer, Southern Railway. These new, and lighter, steel-bodied carriages, rebuilt on the vintage chassis of the earlier wooden-body carriages had several improvements such as wider windows, comfortable cushioned seating, compact fluorescent lights, and a public address system to play light stereo music, or, to make announcements. The coaches also boasted of a cellular-phone charging facility. The Railway Board is said to have sanctioned funds for re-conditioning ten carriages, in the first batch.

The four new carriages were subject to trials on the rack section at Kallar, and were based at Mettupalayam for over two months. It was subsequently used as a rake for a Special Chartered train with British tourists in November 2007, and put to regular use in February 2008, earning encomiums from the tourists and other regular travellers. Also, from 2007, the "Trains at a glance" time tables featured trains on Nilagiri Railway, and internet booking facility was also made available for trains on this line.

## Complacent Railway Authorities and Commuters' Agony

The national highway linking Coonoor with Mettupalayam was closed to traffic for over a month from the end of October 2007, to effect repairs to a steel truss bridge at Kallar (built in 1925 by Jessop & Co., Calcutta); necessitating in diversion of road traffic via a circuitous route. The Railways failed to cash in on this opportunity by operating additional trains between the plains and Coonoor, to alleviate the hardship of tourists and daily commuters, despite there being no bus transport.

## NMR Transferred to Salem Division

Meanwhile, a new railway division was carved out in Southern Railway, known as Salem Division. It was inaugurated by the Railway Minister,

Lalu Prasad on November 1, 2007, and the Nilgiri Mountain Railway (hitherto under Palghat Division), was transferred to this. Salem Divison thus has the rare honour of having the 46-kilometre long World Heritage railway under its jurisdiction. With this, one nurtures the hope that this rack and pinion mountain railway would see better times, not an odyssey to oblivion.

## Inspection Trolley Mishap

In June 2008, an inspection trolley carrying railway personnel and some heavy equipment proceeded down the ghats from Coonoor to a track repair site. Due to poor maintenance, its brakes failed and the trolley sped downhill on the winding track at a great speed. Two of those aboard jumped off but hit rocks on the side of the track and succumbed to their injuries, and the others were badly hurt when the trolley left the track and overturned.

As superstitious beliefs still prevail in the region, a prayer (*yagam*) was conducted by the railway employees at Coonoor, sacrificing a goat to appease the gods (or goddesses) to ensure that such accidents do not happen in future!

## Public Opinion on NMR

Several among the 5000-member strong IRFCA - the Indian Railways Fan Club - opine that more trains should be run between Coimbatore and Mettupalayam, with suitable connecting services between Mettupalayam and Udagamandalam on Nilagiri Railway, because as of now there is just a solitary Nilagiri Passenger each way to connect the Nilagiri Express running between Mettupalayam and Chennai Central. "Freight trains (suspended since February 1982) should also be re-introduced, being a good source of revenue for the Railways," said a member.

Javed from Afghanistan, one among a group of tourists on a train from Mettupalayam said, "My teacher in Bangalore insisted that we should have a trip in this wonderful train. Just to have a feel of the travel, we came to Ooty. It is simply amazing. We are able to see the technical wonders and heritage buildings of the last century."

## Continuing Campaign to Save the NMR

Well, as of now, despite the mountain railway going on a 'periodic holiday', the four passenger coaches of the solitary Nilagiri Passenger, chugging up and down the ghats between Mettupalayam and Udagamandalam are packed to capacity. Do experience the joy of travelling on this World Heritage railway which seems to cry, *"I've lasted another year!"*

As the campaign continues for improving the state of affairs on the Nilgiri Mountain Railway, it is hoped that the Ministry of Railways would also make a sincere effort towards the modernisation of this unique and scenic engineering marvel of the erstwhile British rule in India - the NMR, for posterity. They'd better get cracking fast, before the vintage Swiss-made steam engines decide to call it a day!

Painted on a revetment alongside the rail-track via lush tea gardens at Glendale:

*So many people come and go*

*But the train brings more and more*

*Will they? For how long?*

# New Developments:
# October 2008 to January 2018

As an addendum to this book, the events leading up to the revised edition are definitely not to be missed out.

## 100 Years of the Extension of the
## Nilgiri Mountain Railway from Coonoor to Ootacamund

The Nilgiri Mountain Railway was extended from Coonoor to Ootacamund (Ooty) on October 15, 1908, and as part of the month long celebration of the "Centenary of the Extension of the NMR," a Black Beauty contest was held at Coonoor on October 18, 2008. It was the second such contest in the annals of this mountain railway. On parade were four vintage Swiss steam engines in a grand display of steam and smoke amidst a steady drizzle and moderate fog, creating a phantasmagoric effect. The winner was the oldest steam engine X-37384, built by SLM Winterthur in 1914 and put on service in April 1920. This engine had earlier bagged the prize at the first Black Beauty contest in April 1997 as part of the Centenary of Coonoor Railway Station.

A fifteen member group of tourists from Saint Etienne in France led by their Deputy Mayor Martine Fontanilles arrived by the Nilagiri Passenger, and stated that during their long holiday they had travelled by rail in many parts of the world including Peru and Vietnam. Ms. Fontanilles said that this journey from Mettupalayam would remain fresh in their memory for long, and the scenery en route was breathtaking. She opined that if a steam engine was used throughout the journey from Mettupalayam instead of a diesel locomotive between Coonoor and Udagamandalam, it would enhance the joy.

**Also on this special occasion, my book: NMR – FROM LIFELINE TO OBLIVION was released at the Coonoor Club, and a report appeared in The Hindu newspaper on October 20, 2008. Excerpts from the news report:**

### Role of Local People in Keeping NMR Alive Hailed

With the famed Nilgiri Mountain Railway (NMR) hogging the limelight since last week following the centenary celebrations of its Coonoor-Ooty section being set in motion, a function was organised by the Nilgiris Cultural Association (NCA) and the NMR Society at Coonoor on Friday to release a book on the NMR compiled by a local railway enthusiast V.M. Govind Krishnan.

Presenting the first copy of his book titled 'NMR: From Lifeline to Oblivion' to T. Rangaiah, president, NMR Society, Mr. Krishnan pointed out that but for the protests registered by the local people, the NMR would have been dismantled a long time ago. The proposal to dismantle the line on account of it being uneconomical had been mooted in 1968 and subsequently the NMR had been neglected in many ways.

Stating that his book was a tribute to the relentless campaign of the NMR enthusiasts to keep the services going, he claimed that it was largely due to their efforts that the NMR was declared as a World Heritage Site by the United Nations Educational, Scientific and Cultural Organisation

(UNESCO) a few years ago. The book traces the efforts of the local people to keep the line alive.

Listing the efforts of the NMR Society to prevent dismantling of the line, Mr. Rangaiah said that the first public initiative was the society's celebration of the centenary of Coonoor railway station in 1997, when an imposing permanent iron welcome arch was erected at the threshold of the station and employees were honoured. The society had been relentlessly fighting for the survival of NMR for commercial, tourism and economic purposes, and played a significant role in the organisation of a black beauty contest in April 1997. The NCA president, P.S. Sundar, said that after Independence, services on the NMR line had been suspended as many as 25 times. At times the suspension lasted several months. Many stations had been closed over the years. Though the Southern Railway had put to rest speculation regarding the continuance of the NMR, the line will run into serious problems if new locomotives were not pressed into service soon. The existing ones were nearing the end of their hauling capacity.

On April 26, 2009, The New Indian Express reported, "The Southern Railway is examining the feasibility of operating a special train from Mettupalayam to Ooty during this summer. As a sequel to the great inconvenience faced by tourists because the Nilgiri train has been running late and getting repaired often, officials of the Southern Railway travelled between Mettupalayam and Coonoor to conduct track inspection, study the problems faced, and submit a report to the Railway Ministry on the feasibility of running the existing regular train from May 1."

## Nilgiri Railway – Deteriorating Services and Public Angst

Following frequent steam engine failures on the rack and pinion route between Mettupalayam and Coonoor, a public demonstration was staged at Coonoor in August 2009 urging suitable action to improve the condition of the steam engines in use and ensure proper maintenance, and to procure new ones. Among those who participated were representatives of the Federation of Service Organisations, Coonoor Merchants Association, various consumer outfits, and non-governmental organizations. Parameswaran, convener of the Federation of Service Organisations announced that all was not well with this major tourist attraction which is also a UNESCO World Heritage Site; and pointed out that the manner in which it was being maintained is disturbing to the people of the Nilgiri Hills. "The train frequently developed technical problems while ascending or descending, and those aboard were subjected to considerable inconvenience," he said, and stressed that even though the NMR is extremely popular among the tourists and the Southern Railway is aware of this, nothing tangible has been done to provide better services. A memorandum submitted called for action by the Railway Ministry to get new steam engines, and to set up a railway museum at Ooty.

In a joint memorandum sent in September 2009 to the General Manager-Southern Railway, the State Joint Secretary, Padmanabhan, and the District Secretary, Rajarathinam, pointed out that services on the NMR were far from satisfactory, and despite advancements in technology, the train often suffers a delay of several hours owing to the poor quality of the steam engines and substandard coal to fuel them. The memorandum stated that the explanation given by the railway officials was not convincing and the track and rolling stock required proper maintenance. As a sequel to several representations by the citizens, and the NMR Society, the Railways sanctioned funds to strengthen the track and replace the worn out rails, rack-bars and sleepers. When asked about the long standing proposal to purchase new steam locomotives at a cost of Rs. 100 crore from Switzerland, railway officials said that the plan was shelved because the original company at Winterthur changed hands and had ceased to build steam engines. The railway workshop at Golden Rock, Tiruchirapally, was given the task to build four new oil fired steam engines at Rs. 40 crore, and the first engine was expected to roll out by the end of December 2010.

## High Level Meeting Held at Chennai, on Problems Faced by the NMR

The New Indian Express, Chennai, dated May 29, 2009 reported that the Southern Railway has formulated a two pronged approach to address both track and locomotive issues on the NMR, at a high level meeting held on May 28. An official said, "We intend to complete track renewal for 17 km of the track identified out of the total section, with reconditioning of steel sleepers and manufacture of new rack chairs, which are an integral part of this specialised track structure; and the ballast will be subjected to a process known as deep screening."

## Excerpts from Southern Railway Press Release

After the high level meeting held on May 28, 2009 at the headquarters of Southern Railway in Chennai, a press release was issued, excerpts from which are:

"Maintaining and operating trains on this 100 year old mountain railway system is a challenging task, and like any system that is both unique as well as old, failures do occur.

There have been disruptions in services on the Nilgiri Mountain Railway in the recent past which have been primarily on account of failure of locomotives as well as some track failures. The Railway accords the highest priority to the safe transportation of passengers and no compromises are made on safety. This may lead to cancellation of services which often generate adverse comment since it does cause public inconvenience. In the event of an asset failure, immediate action is taken to restore the asset, ensure its proper functioning and then resume services. This is being done on the Nilgiri Mountain

Railway also. However, Southern Railway does not have a long term action plan, given the cultural and historic value of this railway line."

The release also states, "The Railway has already sanctioned four new steam locomotives which will be manufactured at the Golden Rock Workshop. However, the first of these locomotives will be available after a year or so. Until such time, special efforts have been made to improve the stock of critical spares and to ensure the highest quality of the same. Already two locomotives with oil fired systems have been inducted into the circuit, and it is proposed to convert more locos in a similar fashion."

## Deccan Herald dated November 4, 2009 reports:

### 'Chaiyya Chaiyya' Train Not to Chug Anymore

Nilgiris Mountain Railway (NMR) train of "Chaiyya chaiyya" fame will soon cease to chug, as the good old steam engine is set to give way to diesel locomotives to meet the increasing flow of tourists to the hill resort town of Ooty A series of tests and trials of the diesel locomotive with five coaches was held between Mettupalayam and Hillgrove stations on Saturday, Southern Railway officials said. Use of diesel locomotives on NMR will help in operating more coaches between Mettupalayam and Coonoor, about 20 km downhill from Udhagamandalam, than in steam operated trains, thereby catering to more tourists and locals.

Film director Mani Ratnam shot the popular 'Chaiyya chaiyaa' song of his film "Dil Se" featuring Shah Rukh Khan and Malaika Arora atop a train on this line. Also, the reliability of train services can be improved, thereby avoiding delays in train services, the officials said. NMR passing through picturesque mountains has been carrying tourists to the queen of hill stations for over a century.

## Oil Fired Engine Snag, Crew Members Suffer Burns

On July 5, 2010, a snag on the oil fired steam engine X-37391 halted the train near Runneymede en route from Mettupalayam to Ooty. A coal fired relief engine was rushed from Mettupalayam to the spot. While on its way to Coonoor, pulling the stranded train along with its faulty engine, a sudden gust of steam in the oil fired engine caused moderate burns to the loco driver A. Premdas, the assistant driver Kennedy and fitter Dorai, and they had to be hospitalised at Coonoor.

## More Coal Engines Undergo Conversion to Oil Firing

Two more vintage Swiss steam engines were sent for conversion to oil firing at Golden Rock, Tiruchirapally, in view of the paucity of good quality coal to fuel the engines; but inexplicably the first successfully converted engine X-37395 was re-converted back to coal burner in August 2009. It was used to haul a "Heritage Special" between Coonoor and Ooty carrying 39 mentally and physically challenged children selected from three institutions on the occasion of NMR Day celebrations. The children undoubtedly were thrilled and thoroughly enjoyed the gesture by the Railways. In March 2011 the same engine was seen in a forlorn state outside the Loco Shed at Coonoor with the words, "World Heritage Site," painted on it!

## Trial Run of YDM-4 Diesel Engines on the Rack Railway

It was reported in The Hindu, Chennai, dated Nov. 6, 2009 that with track strengthening works along the 46-km stretch of the metre-gauge Nilgiri Railway nearing completion, railway engineers have decided to temporarily replace the steam engines with diesel engines. According to the Chief Mechanical Engineer (Southern Railway) V. Carmelus, "All seven steam engines imported from Switzerland had outlived their efficiency period, and despite efforts to maintain the system the steam engines have failed on many occasions, causing inconvenience to passengers. The Research Design and Standards Organisation (RDSO), Lucknow, and the Commissioner of Railway Safety have cleared the proposal to operate trains with twin diesel engines. With improved track condition and enhanced hauling power of diesel engines, the speed of the trains will go up from the present 13 km/h in the critical Kallar - Coonoor (20 km) section."

Subsequently, attempts were made to run a trial-train on the rack and pinion route using a YDM-4 diesel engine - which is not equipped with the pinion mechanism to operate on the rack railway! Trial runs over a short distance with an empty train were conducted at the start of the rack section from Kallar, with a YDM-4 diesel locomotive, banked by a steam engine. Later, a trial was done using twin diesel engines for more power to overcome the gradient. The trials ended in failure as the locomotives stalled after reaching the steeper gradient on the track.

Ivan Baxter, the Guard on a trial train confided, "I was scared when the train stalled and started sliding back; but with dexterity the descent was controlled and the train was brought safely back to Kallar." Subsequently, further trials were discontinued as a safety measure, and also because of a sudden onset of inclement weather and heavy rainfall announcing the arrival of the north east monsoon. Thereafter, the YDM-4 diesel locomotives are used only on the non-rack section of the Nilgiri railway between Coonoor and Udagamandalam.

## Torrential Rains, Landslides, Massive Devastation

All access by road and rail to the entire Nilgiri district was cut off by unprecedented heavy rains between Nov. 8 and 11, 2009, and over 30 km of the 46 km railway track suffered extensive damage. Many roads caved in and several new houses built on steep hillsides collapsed in the district.

It was impossible to reach the sites of landslide damage on the railway owing to continuous heavy rains. Later, a team of engineering officials led by the Assistant Divisional Engineer, Podanur, trekked along the railway track to assess the devastation caused to the bridges and the track. Top honchos of Southern Railway were briefed about the extent of destruction caused by rain and landslides, to commence track rehabilitation work. The Railways estimated that the terrain was vulnerable to landslides, and since 1899 when it was operational the NMR services had been hit more than 25 times by landslides. The Railways had strengthened retention walls adjoining the tracks and also put up retention walls at many vulnerable places on the route.

## Track Restoration, and New Bridges Built

A large workforce was deployed to expedite the restoration work, but the work was hampered by the hostile terrain that lacked an approach road to transport men and material to the breached spots. Over a hundred landslips and fallen trees had to be cleared by laboriously transporting earthmovers, manpower and other equipment stage by stage by rail only. Three bridges had to be re-built anew between Hillgrove and Runneymede after mudslides and massive chunks of rock rolling downhill destroyed the track, girders, and stone-pillars of the original structures. The feat of reconstructing the track, bridges, and launching girders was started at a considerable risk, because only one steam engine was stationed at Mettupalayam to operate the train carrying the equipment. Fortuitously, a steam engine X-37392, after conversion to oil firing at Tiruchirapally, reached Mettupalayam on January 28, 2010 to offer assistance in hauling more equipment to quicken the pace of track restoration. The men on the restoration team had to face an unexpected hurdle i.e. wild elephants. The officials found that a concrete mixer was tossed down a deep ravine by a herd of pachyderms which made a nocturnal visit, and damaged freshly repaired portions at the sites. Abutment walls had to be rebuilt after elephants stomped over them.

A major damage on the rail route between Coonoor and Ootacamund occurred near Aravankadu, where the earth beneath the track was washed away by torrential rain on Nov. 9, 2009, necessitating the erection of a new bridge to span the 100 metre gap, using girders supported atop steel cribs. There was a small culvert at this spot till then. Long girders brought from Tiruchirapally were cut and re-sized to transport them by road from Mettupalayam via Kotagiri only after this ghat road was temporarily restored by clearing several landslips; because the rail and road routes from Mettupalayam were totally snapped. The girders were cut to enable transport by road via hairpin bends on the narrow and circuitous route to the breach spot. Trains services between Coonoor and Ooty were resumed from Jan. 5, 2010 over the temporary structure, till permanent concrete pillars were built in June 2010. The Mettupalayam - Coonoor route was reopened from May 1, 2010 after 156 days of stoppage, at an expense of Rs. 12 crore and 4.48 lakh man hours (400 x 8 hrs day x 140 days = 4,48,000 man hours). It is a matter of pride that the railway authorities took up the track restoration work with such zeal, and accomplished the feat a fortnight ahead of schedule. A senior railway official commented, "The NMR is a World Heritage Site and it is a prestigious service for Indian Railways and an engineering marvel. So, it is important to restore train services as soon as possible."

## Steam Engine Catches Fire

Owing to lack of coal, only those engines converted to oil firing were in use on the Coonoor - Mettupalayam route from 2010. The converted to furnace oil powered Swiss-built steam engine X-37391 powering the passenger train from Mettupalayam caught fire on September 1, 2010 near the level-crossing at Coonoor, causing a massive disruption to road traffic for over an hour, till it was pulled to the station, 300 metres away by a YDM-4 diesel locomotive which was to take over for the run to Ooty. At other times, the oil fired steam engine pushing the passenger train suddenly switched off midway stranding the train in the dense forest en route. As attempts to restart the engine failed, a relief engine was sent from Coonoor to rescue the train resulting in cancellation of the corresponding train service. Occasionally, even the relief engine developed snags, inconveniencing all aboard the train for several hours.

On October 24, 2010, the train to Ooty was cancelled midway following a technical snag in the steam engine. Owing to snapping of a rod in the engine, the train stopped midway at the Kallar level crossing gate near the start of the ghat section. About 200 tourists in the train were taken to Udagamandalam in buses, and steps were taken to tow the train back to Mettupalayam. Buses and cars might be able to transport people efficiently and quickly, but for most visitors to the Nilgiri Hills the leisurely railway journey is more important than the destination.

## White Paper on NMR Safety Sought

The Coonoor-based Federation of Service Organisations has asked people from all walks of life in the Nilgiris to strengthen the ongoing efforts to make the railway authorities improve the functioning of the Nilgiri Mountain Railway. The New Indian Express dated September 8, 2010 reported that rail enthusiasts apprehended the fate of the Nilgiri railway and demanded that Southern Railway should come out with a white paper explaining its measures to assure safe and sure travel to tourists on the NMR. A concerned citizen remarked, "They have allowed engines to outlive their capacity. Initially, the train ran with five compartments and one luggage van with 20-tonne capacity which was subsequently reduced to four compartments and a guard-cum-luggage van with 4-tonne capacity, and now the train is reduced to just three compartments! Authorities are proposing a toy-train experience with steam engine, operating within the Ooty station yard, which raises doubt on the survival of this mountain railway!"

As the working fleet of steam engines on the NMR was reduced to just two, the "Summer Special" train could not be run for three consecutive years despite heavy inflow of visitors to Nilgiri Hills during the summer season; and bus and cab operators enriched themselves. The steam engines suffered mechanical failures like piston rod breakage, lack of sufficient steam pressure, and other technical snags. Occasionally, water-pipes at Adderley – the first filling station way up the ghat from Kallar, were found to be damaged by foraging wild elephants, and the train was forced to return to Kallar. Train services between Coonoor and Udhagamandalam were not affected as YDM-4 bio-diesel locomotives were used, being a non-rack route on a mild gradient.

On February 25, 2011, the train from Ooty to Mettupalayam was cancelled beyond Coonoor as the steam engine assigned to haul the train developed a snag which could not be rectified, and no spare engine in working order was available. The passengers almost came to blows with the Station Manager and other railway staff at Coonoor, as they had to connect the Nilgiri Express to Chennai. The passengers calmed down after the Railways arranged two buses to drop them at the railway station in Mettupalayam.

## First India-Built Steam Engine for Nilgiri Railway

On February 19, 2011 the first of four new oil-fired steam engines - built at Golden Rock Workshop (GRW), Tiruchirapally, entered the fleet to supplement the dwindling number of vintage Swiss steam engines. This is the first time that the workshop has embarked on the task of manufacturing oil-fired metre gauge steam locomotives. When brought to Coonoor on its own steam on Feb 26, 2011, Kullan, a mechanic at the loco shed said, "We hope that the engine will run smoothly. It is a big achievement that the engine was built in Tiruchi." An engineer involved in the project to build the engine from century old plans said, "The track suitability and other technical details have to be checked, and trials will be held on the Coonoor - Mettupalayam rack railway section before it is ready for regular use. The new engine has been provided with pilot and primary burners with separate tanks to hold about 850 litres of diesel and 2,250 litres of furnace oil." The claimed hauling capacity of this engine was 97.6 tonnes at a speed of 30 km/h in the plains and 15 km an hour on the gradient. After a complete health-check at the Coonoor loco shed and a few trial runs, it was assigned road number X-37396, and inducted into service. While flagging off the new engine at Coonoor on March 24, 2011, an official of the Southern Railway claimed, "Quality wise the new engine is better than the original." He also said that the second new engine would join the fleet after a few months.

A report in The Hindu mentions: "Stating that a rack-and-pinion system made the NMR unique, he said that X Class locomotives had been specially designed for it." Since the existing seven X Class locomotives, made in Switzerland, were between 60 and 100 years old, the Railway Board had given the nod for the manufacture of four new X Class locomotives at a cost of Rs. 10 crore each. Considerable efforts were made to import the locomotives. However, they went in vain due to the unique design and prohibitive costs. A Swiss company had quoted Rs. 40 crore for manufacturing one engine. The GRW started work on the first engine in 2009. With spare parts being made in various places including in Coimbatore, the engine was put together at a cost of Rs. 3.75 crore. The locomotive has been subjected to extensive load trials on the NMR line to ensure trouble-free service.

Having entered regular service on the line, the new engine also suffered breakdowns and lack of steam pressure twice within three months of use, prompting the Railways to cancel the solitary passenger train service on the Coonoor - Mettupalayam section, without notice on some days, owing to lack of a 'dependable steam engine'.

## Derailment of a Carriage

On May 1, 2011 a minor derailment of a wheel of the carriage attached to the engine caused the train to Mettupalayam to get stuck on the ghat below Coonoor, and all aboard 'enjoyed a trek' through the forest, with their luggage, to reach the road and board buses toward Mettupalayam. Following this incident, train services remained cancelled for nine days at a stretch for repairs to the track and rack bars. On May 10, the train from Mettupalayam powered by the new engine developed a snag and stranded the train near Runneymede, and the passengers were again forced to trek in rain over a furlong to reach the road. As a relief engine from Coonoor was sent to bring the empty train, the corresponding service to Mettupalayam, and the following day's train from Mettupalayam remained cancelled.

## Steam Engine Failures Inconvenience Travellers

Bhaswaran, a freelance photographer from Calcutta who travelled with his family from Mettupalayam just to experience the journey on the Nilgiri Mountain Railway said, "I found the steam engine losing power at least four times during the run, it had to stop, regain steam and then push up again. I felt the condition of the engines was not at all good, but we somehow managed to reach Coonoor!" On May 24, 2011 the train faced a major technical problem. A travel weary tourist exclaimed, "It took us nearly eight hours to reach Coonoor from Mettupalayam, a distance of

27 km. The train stopped at about 30 places on the ghat section on its way uphill due to lack of steam pressure, and this exhausted the water and furnace oil in the steam engine."

"In the last six months, the train has broken down more than 25 times, despite the introduction of a new indigenous oil-fired steam engine to replace the ageing Swiss X class engines; raising a serious concern for the survival of this unique marvel of engineering skill," opined T. Rangaiah, President, NMR Society. As newspapers highlighted the continuing steam engine failures, the General Manager-Southern Railway, Deepak Krishan, rushed to Coonoor on May 25, 2011 with a team of mechanical engineers and senior officials to take stock of the deterioration in train services on the Nilgiri Mountain Railway owing to snag prone steam engines. The general manager and his team also had a taste of aborted running and were forced to travel by road from Kallar, as the steam engine attached to their "Inspection Special" train failed en route just before the start of the rack section. At Coonoor, a memorandum was handed over to Deepak Krishan by the Federation of Service Organisations to apprise him of the deteriorating state of the NMR, and to take steps to ensure trouble free service henceforth. In a report in The Hindu, railway enthusiasts expressed apprehension that if matters concerning the NMR were allowed to drift, in a matter of time they would get out of hand; and suggested that expert help should be sought from abroad.

On May 29, 2011 when the train from Mettupalayam was stranded en route, inconveniencing passengers for almost four hours, a railway official explained, "Oil and water leaked out and so the oil fired loco failed to produce sufficient steam to push the train uphill. The engine failed suddenly near Adderley."

At the Railway Board in New Delhi, an official claimed ignorance, as per a report in The Times of India, Chennai, which read, "The matter of frequent breakdowns on the NMR has not been brought to my notice. This is the first time I am hearing of it. I will look into the matter. However, the operational control of NMR lies with the zonal railway," said Manu Goyal, Executive Director - Heritage, Indian Railways.

## "Save Nilgiri Mountain Railway" Campaign Continues

Frequent disruption and suspension of train services on the rack section owing to steam engine failures prompted over a 100 NGOs along with other concerned citizens to hold a demonstration on June 13, 2011, with the participation of NMR Society, press-persons, trade organisations and NMR enthusiasts; under the banner "NMR Protection Committee" to organize a campaign to 'Save Nilgiri Mountain Railway.' A Member of Parliament from Erode, A. Ganeshamurthy, said, "It is a prestigious heritage line, and the Railway Ministry must protect it at all costs," and promised to raise the issue in the Lok Sabha. Going by tourist reactions, it is clear that the business potential for the NMR is enormous, but the Railways must act quickly to tap it. If it does not, this technological wonder will die a natural death by simply running out of steam engines.

"Unannounced cancellations apart from disappointing many tourists, raised the frustration level among the people of the Nilgiris who were looking forward to a marked improvement after members of the Save NMR Campaign held a demonstration at Coonoor railway station." said Natarajan, founder of Heritage Steam Chariot Trust. Referring to its recognition as a World Heritage site by UNESCO, the convenor, Indian National Trust for Art, Culture and Heritage (INTACH), the Nilgiris Chapter, Geetha Srinivasan, said that the mountain railway was the sole reason for a large number of tourists from India and abroad visiting the Nilgiri Hills. "It is high time the authorities concerned sit up and take note of this fact," she said. The secretary, Nilgiri Hotels and Restaurants

Association, N. Chandrashekar said: "Many of the tourists want to see or experience all the attractions in the Nilgiris in as little a time as possible. If they happen to be on a train which runs into problems on the way, their sightseeing plans will be thrown out of gear." He cautioned that if warning signs are continued to be ignored, the mountain railway will be consigned to the pages of history in a matter of time.

## A Fruit Replica of Coonoor Railway Station

At the 53$^{rd}$ Annual Fruit Show held on May 29, 2011 at the 137 years old Sim's Park in Coonoor, the main attraction was a life-size fruit replica of Coonoor railway station - a heritage building. The replica measured 35'x15'x15' and was composed of 25000 *musambis* (sweet lime). A visitor, N. Wood, jokingly remarked, "Lay the rails and keep a steam engine and a carriage next year because the train may not be there!"

As the Nilgiri Mountain Railway turned 113 on June 15, 2011, a British couple in a tour group aboard the train from Mettupalayam to Coonoor gushed, "It was an incredible once in a lifetime experience — our first in a steam engine!" For every tourist visiting the Nilgiris, travelling on the NMR at least in one direction is a dream. The Nilgiri train that runs through the most beautiful parts of the Western Ghats incurs a staggering loss of Rs. 6 crore per annum, and overall expenditure on Nilgiri Mountain Railway runs to Rs. 24 crore a year. Yet, the trains run with full occupancy with an eclectic mix of tourists from all over the world. As per railway records all the five mountain railways in India are running at a loss. In 2008, almost Rs. 2 crore was spent on restoring the rail track. A new oil-fired steam engine built at a cost of Rs. 3.75 crore to replace the original Swiss X class engines was inaugurated in 2011.

Southern Railway authorities announced on August 17, 2011 that the second new oil fired steam engine that is being built at the Golden

Rock Workshop for the Nilgiri Mountain Railway is likely to roll out by October 2011. After three deadlines had elapsed, it is yet to arrive on the scene. Rumours of permanent closure of the Nilgiri Railway surfaced again toward the end of August 2011 after Southern Railway stopped the reservation facility on the NMR from October 5, 2011, and the on-line booking sites showed 'Train cancelled'. Wallace from Newcastle-upon-Tyne who was planning to travel in November 2011 pointed this out, as his travel agent told him that the Nilgiri Railway was to be permanently closed!

## Salem Division Dismisses Rumours of Closure

Following public outcry and reports in the newspapers, G.V. Venkatesan, Public Relations Officer - Salem Division on September 6, 2011 said, "There is no idea to shut down the line for whatever reason. The only thing is that due to technical challenges like landslide etc., the train services are getting disrupted. So, to avoid difficulty to the reserved passengers, Salem Division is making alternative arrangements in the event of any stoppage of the train. So, the train services are on as such, and not cancelled."

The Hindu dated September 8, 2011 reported that "Southern Railway officials have dismissed as speculative and baseless, reports about winding up of the Nilgiri Mountain Railway (NMR) and suspension of trains from October 5," and explained that this confusion arose because the reservation facility was to be stopped temporarily so that those with confirmed tickets were not disappointed by sudden cancellation of trains.

On September 13, 2011 the train from Mettupalayam to Ootacamund powered by an oil fired steam engine ran out of steam on the ghat, and a relief coal-fired engine was despatched from Coonoor. The three-carriage train with two engines, full of tourists, was seen entering Coonoor nearly three hours late powered by the relief engine at the front. This delayed the corresponding service to Mettupalayam by an hour.

## Runneymede Set to Become a Tourist Spot

The Hindu dated October 2, 2011 reported that a long standing demand to exploit the tourism potential of the long closed Runneymede station on the NMR was likely to be fulfilled. The Heritage Steam Chariot Trust, Ooty, had been urging the railway authorities to develop Runneymede because the station is located in a scenic spot below Coonoor; and if the station was re-opened and special trips were run, both eco and heritage tourism would get a boost. The Divisional Railway Manager, P.N. Ram visited the station and stated that the proposal could be considered only if it satisfied various parameters. He said that railway engineers would also examine the reasons for the mountain train developing mechanical problems while running between Coonoor and Mettupalayam. It was felt that the priority focus should be on pressing into service adequate number of reliable and efficient locomotives.

## New India-built Oil Fired X Class Steam Engines

The second indigenously built oil-fired steam engine X-37397 was rolled out on Feb 7, 2012 ar Golden Rocks Works, Tiruchirapally Weighing nearly 50 tonnes, the 'X' class metre gauge steam loco has been provided with welded type boiler for the first time procured through outsourcing, The workshop manager, P. Mahesh, said, "The new steam engine is fired by furnace oil, a type of petroleum by-product which is neither petrol, diesel or kerosene. Earlier, the British used coal instead of oil, but now, as the Indian coal does not have the requisite caloristic value, we have to resort to this furnace-type oil." This new engine was put into service on March 20, 2012.

The third oil fired steam engine X-37398 costing Rs. 3.7 crore was flagged off at Golden Rock Workshop on March 8, 2013, and after extensive trials it was inducted into service on the Nilgiri Railway in April 2013. Similar to the second loco dispatched in March last year, the third loco has also been fitted with all welded boiler.

The fourth and final oil fired steam engine X-37399 was rolled out at Tiruchirapally on March 6, 2014, and put on trials from Mettupalayam. It entered service on the line on March 24, 2014.

### An excerpt from The Times of India, Thursday Nov. 29, 2012:

### Boulder Falls on Ooty Train, School Girl Hurt

As part of their excursion programme, a group of school girls from Kozhikode in Kerala were travelling from Mettupalayam to Ooty on Wednesday. Around 40 students from SKV Girls School in Kozhikode were accommodated in one of the compartments. At around 9 A.M, when the train was crossing Adderley, a huge boulder rolled down. As the roof of the train was damaged by the boulder, a fragment fell inside the compartment causing minor injury to a student. Station master, Babu at Coonoor said, "The cause of the accident is not known. Maybe some animals on the hills above the track might have pushed down the rock."

### Tatkal Booking System on NMR

On December 26, 2013 Tatkal system of booking tickets was introduced in the Nilgiri Mountain Railway, for which advance reservation system is already in force. Out of the 90 second class seats, nine seats have been alloted for Tatkal and charges would be Rs. 40 per ticket for the Train numbers 56136/56137.

## 9th Convention of Indian Railways Fan Club (IRFCA) – Ooty 2014

At the 9th Convention of the Indian Railways Fan Club (IRFCA) held for the first time at Ooty in February 2014, Rakesh Misra, General Manager-Southern Railway said that the railway authorities often benefit from the out-of-the-box ideas of the rail enthusiasts, and their feedback is given due importance. He added that "The maintenance of the NMR was not only a science but also an art," and alternate arrangements have been made to overcome shortage of skilled manpower because most maintenance staff on Nilgiri Railway had retired.

## Joint Efforts Needed to Promote Nilgiri Mountain Railway

There is a need for joint action to protect and promote the Nilgiri Mountain Railway, said Rajesh Agarwal, Deputy General Manager, North East Frontier Railway, at Ootacamund on Monday March 10, 2014.

He said that the district administration, the Department of Tourism, the Forest Department, the Indian National Trust for Art, Culture and Heritage, and the railways should join hands for the purpose. The Nilgiri Mountain Railway and the Darjeeling Himalayan Railway were unique railway systems, and should be projected properly, and the stations on way could be improved. Mr. Rajesh Agarwal was of the view that the services on the line could be doubled or tripled, and the mountain railway could be used to attract high spending tourists.

The former Chairman of the Atomic Energy Commission, M.R. Srinivasan, said that the rare rack and pinion system of the mountain railway should be showcased to visitors. The convener, INTACH, Geetha Srinivasan, said that ugly structures should not be allowed to come up along the line between Mettupalayam and Udhagamandalam. It was suggested at the interaction that a Nilgiri logo should be brought out with a picture of the mountain railway.

## Proposal to Run Summer Special Trains Rejected

On a visit by the General Manager-Southern Railway, Rakesh Misra, to Coonoor on April 22, 2013, he clarified that there was no proposal to run summer specials during the current season on the Nilgiri Mountain Railway (NMR) line between Ooty and Mettupalayam. He told presspersons that lack of adequate coaches was among the reasons, and said that after dusk it is risky to run trains on the sector due to the movement of wild elephants. To a question, he replied that though the NMR is uneconomical, it will not be closed. It has been recognised as a World Heritage Site, and it will be maintained properly.

On March 23, 2014, the new General Manager-Southern Railway, Vashista Johri, said, "The conventional coal fired locomotives had to be replaced with furnace-oil fired engines as it was not possible to ensure a steady supply of high quality coal in small quantities. Considering the enormous heritage value, the mountain railway should be preserved with some modern amenities." He also said that since parts of the line were traditional elephant crossing areas all aspects including the likelihood of train-elephant collision had to be considered before exploring the possibility of increasing the number of services.

On May 13, 2015, the Southern Railway decided to run the solitary train between Mettupalayam and Ooty with four carriages instead of three to cater to the increasing number of tourists. Requests to run additional trains have been futile so far. The additional coach will help 56 more travellers move from Mettupalayam to Coonoor and a few more from there to Ooty as a fifth coach gets attached and the locomotive gets changed from the furnace oil-powered steam engine to a YDM-4 diesel locomotive at Coonoor. The present composition of the train will be one first class coach, two second class coaches and a luggage-cum-guard van. The Southern Railway had to reduce the number of coaches to three a few years ago after the train from Mettupalayam was either delayed or stranded mid-forest because the furnace-oil powered locomotive struggled to push up the carriages.

Do not forget the fact that the original coal-fired Swiss-built engines pushed six carriages uphill till mid-1970s. Later, due to ageing engines the passenger trains were reduced in number to just one train each way today, on the rack railway between Mettupalayam and Coonoor; and goods trains ceased to ply after lorry transport took over.

## Hopper Wagons

Hopper wagons were never seen on Nilgiri Railway. However, in June 2016, two such metre gauge hopper wagons were brought to Coonoor from North Eastern Railway, Gorakhpur, Uttar Pradesh, after tracks were closed for conversion to broad gauge. For use on the Nilgiri line, a hand brake gear was fitted along with a pressure gauge, and a hard metal seat for a brakesman. In mid 2016, one more modified hopper wagon from Northern Frontier Railway was brought to Coonoor following gauge conversion in the State of Assam.

## NMR Museum Opened at Mettupalayam

On October 7, 2015, the Salem Division of Southern Railway inaugurated the NMR Museum at Mettupalayam station, where travellers would be able to get a peek into the history behind one of the country's most scenic mountain trips. People who have booked a trip on NMR can just cross the platform in Mettupalayam station and take a few minutes to look around the museum, which reveals the story behind the railway set up during the British rule. The museum has on display a historic steam locomotive, manufactured in Switzerland, that was used for the service since 1925 (engine number X-37389), a model of the unique rack and pinion system track among other models. Other attractions include a miniature model of an X class locomotive, a wooden model of an old engine model, a few of the earlier tickets and an old crane used during construction of the track. "We have also displayed some old photographs taken during the construction of the track in the 19$^{th}$ century, the first inaugural journeys and a map of the route, so visitors understand it before they embark on the journey," said Shubhranshu, Divisional Railway Manager - Salem Division.

The museum, located in a large shed built on a disused coal dump, has some colourful paintings by railway staff on the exterior walls, one of them based on my 2012-photograph depicting a view of a passenger train at Runneymede station and the newly developed floral garden, Kattery Park, from atop the hill.

## XIII National Steam Congress, New Delhi

At the 13$^{th}$ National Steam Congress organised by the Indian Steam Railway Society (ISRS) on November 21, 2015, the theme for the conference was Nilgiri Mountain Railway, and the function was attended by senior railway officials and rail enthusiasts, including the working president of ISRS and chairman cum managing director -Air India, Ashwani Lohani, and David Mead from Darjeeling Himalayan Railway Society, United Kingdom. A cake featuring the X-class rack and adhesion steam engine operating on Nilgiri Railway was cut on the occasion.

"The unique sounds, the rocking gait, the shrill whistle, the throbbing body and an open design are features that impart an irresistible charm to these black beauties," said Ashwani Lohani. By way of explaining, he said 'Why talk of steam now?' It is the same "charm of these black beauties, and the fire in the belly," and die-hard steam enthusiasts are pushing for the growth of a niche tourism segment in the country known as "Steam Heritage Tourism" so "children know what our heritage is."

## The Hindu dated Dec 03. 2015 reports:

### 60-Year-Old Swiss Loco Given Fresh Lease of Life

Thanks to the technical expertise of the Golden Rock Railway Workshop here, the oil-fired loco has been completely refurbished for operation in Mettupalayam-Coonoor metre gauge hilly terrain. Manufactured by Winterthur Swiss Locomotives and put into service in 1952, the X class steam engine No. 37391 came for periodic overhaul sometime ago at the Golden Rock workshop which has manufactured and despatched new oil fired locos for the NMR section. Originally, the locomotive was coal fired equipped with riveted type boilers, cast iron cylinders, and mild steel water tank. During the second overhaul carried out in 2007, the loco's firing system was converted into oil firing. Workshop authorities told *The Hindu* that this was the third overhaul of the loco at the Golden Rock workshop, which is engaged in a slew of activities including overhaul of diesel locomotives and passenger coaches.

As part of the revamp, the loco weighing nearly 50 tonnes has now been fitted with all – welded boiler for better hauling capacity and improved performance. The mild steel water tanks had been replaced with a couple of non-corrosive stainless steel tanks with its total capacity being 4,000 litres, officials said. The cabin has been fitted with speedometer — another new feature in the loco which had been given a fresh coat of polyurethane painting in its exteriors to give it an aesthetic look. The loco has been provided with twin beam lighting in the front and the rear sides for better illumination and visibility for the loco pilots replacing the dome lights earlier.

A team of technical personnel had worked for nearly eight months to refurbish the loco without disturbing its heritage look, said officials and added that trial runs had been conducted inside the workshop. The refurbished loco was despatched by road to Mettupalayam and put on trial before it was operated on the 27-km stretch between Mettupalayam and Coonoor. The loco could chug at a speed of 30 km an hour on plains and 13 km an hour in the gradient. Declared by UNESCO as a World Heritage Site, the 46-kilometre NMR is a unique metre gauge hill railway with rack and pinion system in place.

## Souvenir Shops Opened

Souvenir shops were opened in 2016 at Mettupalayam, Coonoor and Udagamandalam to vend curios, key-rings and other items such as mugs, pocket-watches and train models, both in metal and cardboard. The cheapest items start at less than Rs. 50. The items are supplied to the stations by the National Rail Museum in New Delhi. These shops were reported to be doing brisk business since they were opened, but the shop in Coonoor station was shut down after a year owing to low patronage. "The NMR engine and train models will hopefully reach us before the beginning of the next peak season." said Pramod, Station Manager, Udagamandalam.

## 11th Anniversary of World Heritage Site Celebrated

On July 16, 2016, NMR celebrated the 11th Anniversary of its recognition as a UNESCO World Heritage site. To mark the occasion, Nilgiri

Documentation Centre distributed the special key chains to the travellers with the picture of the NMR on one side and short description of it on the other. Stating that heritage value of NMR should be reiterated constantly, Dharmalingam Venugopal, director of Nilgiri Documentation Centre, regretted that not enough was being done. While heritage assets of much lesser value were promoted with enthusiasm world over, the NMR, a live heritage, was not adequately promoted. He suggested setting up of a local NMR Heritage Committee with railway and local people participation with clear objectives and necessary funds to promote NMR, which is bound to attract more and more travellers. He also said that making available suitable brochures, maps and souvenirs for the visitors, and setting up a NMR Interpretation Centre at Ooty within the station premises explaining the history, technology and durability of NMR would be a great attraction to tourists and locals. Udagamandalam Station Master Promod, members of the visiting Alpine Mountain Association, Switzerland, the correspondent of Nazareth Convent, Sister Stella Baltazar and Badaga elders Dhona Gowder and M. Nataraj participated.

## Replacement of Metal Bridges

In October 2016 it was decided that the beautiful metal bridges that span sections of the Nilgiri Mountain Railway (NMR) route from Mettupalayam to Coonoor are to be replaced with concrete structures in order to strengthen them against landslides. The new bridges are being installed as the old metal bridges have become corroded and have become structurally unsound. Officials from the Salem Division of the Southern Railway said that of the seventeen bridges that were to be replaced, work had been completed on six. The existing metal bridges that were a few decades old were to be systematically replaced with pre-fabricated concrete structures at an estimated cost of Rs. 1.5 crore.

The replacement work could impact the train schedules, according to the sources. Even the iron sleepers on the tracks are corroding, and the Railways intend replacing the old iron sleepers with concrete ones. K. Natrajan, founder of Heritage Steam Chariot Trust, said that the move to replace the existing steel bridges with concrete structures was welcome from a safety standpoint, but Southern Railway could showcase parts of the older bridges, or an entire section in a museum, so that they could be preserved for posterity.

## Vintage Swiss-Built Steam Engines Withdrawn to Be Displays

As on September 1, 2017, most of the remaining vintage Swiss-built steam engines on the Nilgiri Mountain Railway have been withdrawn from service, and the oil firing equipment removed to restore the original look, and sent as displays to other cities.

## Here Is a List:

- X-37385: At National Rail Museum, Delhi - from 1990.

- X-37390: At Coonoor Station, Tamil Nadu - June 16, 1999, and was moved from the entrance to the station to a new pedestal near the Steam Loco Shed on Nov 15, 2017.

- X-37389 (1925): At Nilgiri Mountain Railway Museum, Mettupalayam, Tamil Nadu - Oct. 7, 2015, is now moved to a pedestal outside Coimbatore station on Aug 9, 2017.

- X-37393 (1950): At Regional Rail Museum, Perambur, Tamil Nadu - Dec. 2014

- X-37395 (1952): At Rail Museum, Tiruchirapally, Tamil Nadu - March 10, 2016

- X-37384 (1914): In service from April 10, 1920, coal fired, and retired in perfect working order in 2016. It could replace the engine moved to Coimbatore from NMR Museum, Mettupalayam.

- X-37386 (1918): In service from April 10, 1921, converted to oil firing in March 2011, withdrawn from service in mid-2016, is now on display at Udagamandalam from Noveember 02, 2017.

# Working Steam Engines on NMR

### Two Swiss-Built Steam Engines

Built by Schweizerische Lokomotiv und Maschinenfabrik (SLM), Winterthur, Switzerland, between 1949, and put into service in 1952.

X-37391 (1949) - in service from Nov 08, 1952, converted to oil firing in 2007, and completely refurbished in Dec. 2015 at Tiruchy (after a fire mishap at Coonoor level crossing gate on Sep. 1, 2010)

X-37392 (1949) - in service from Dec 20, 1952, converted to oil firing in January 2010.

### Four India-Built Steam Engines

Built by Golden Rock Workshop, Tiruchirapally (2011–2014) - because importing new engines were very expensive.

- X-37396 (2011) – with riveted boiler
- X-37397 (2012) – with welded boiler
- X-37398 (2013) – with welded boiler
- X-37399 (2014) – with welded boiler

A few YDM-4 diesel locomotives rendered surplus due to gauge conversion from metre gauge (1000 mm) to broad gauge (1676 mm) on mainline routes in the plains now ply between Coonoor and Ooty on the non-rack route with mild gradients. It is indeed surprising that a completely new diesel engine with a rack-and pinion mechanism has not been specially manufactured for this route by any of the workshops of Indian Railways till now.

### Excerpts from The Pioneer, New Delhi, dated October 9, 2017:

### Railways to Move Mountains to Revive Tourism

Railway Ministry has decided to go in for aggressive promotion and marketing of Rail Tourism through the seven mountain trains across the country. However, safety has been accorded the topmost priority, and the Railway Board has directed the authorities to ensure better upkeep of stations and rail infrastructure like bridges and signals en route the hill trains. The Railway Board convened a special meeting on the hill trains with the stakeholders. It was decided to give utmost priority to safety, cleanliness and smooth operations. The Railways also decided to bring awareness among the people and others like film and television producers for usage of this priceless memento built a century ago by the Britishers.

"Special focus will now be given on rail tourism which was ignored for quite some time. Tourism has immense potential within the Indian Railways network. All the mountain trains will be refurbished and we will offer these services for functions and special events at a very attractive price. Some of our hill trains are world heritage." said a senior rail official. The mountain trains whose safety and renewed comforts have been given priority are Darjeeling Himalayan Railway, Nilgiri Mountain Railway, Kalka-Shimla, Neral-Matheran, Kangra Valley Railway and the newest addition in this segment are Jammu-Baramulla line to the Kashmir valley and Lumding-Badarpur section in the north-eastern India.

## Engine Failures Reappear After a Lull

Engine failure incidents were not heard of on the Nilgiri line for the past few years, but stray incidents in 2016–17 proved to be a reminder of the frequent technical snags on steam engines in the years 2008–2011.

On May 11, 2016, on the climb beyond Kallar toward Coonoor the engine's pushing power became so weak that the train had to be stopped at nearly ten places after Kallar on the rack-and-pinion hill track, and soon thereafter the engine could not move forward as furnace oil also got exhausted. A relief engine was brought from Coonoor to rescue the train and its passengers, who reached their destination late by four hours.

On April 25, 2017, the steam engine lost its pushing power on the ascent from Kallar, and after several halts en route it ended its journey at Hillgrove. A relief engine from Coonoor hauled the train after a delay of a few hours, inconveniencing all aboard.

On May 22, 2017, on the way between Mettupalayam and Coonoor, the engine lost steam power and had to halt many times on the rack railway route and reached Coonoor late by two hours.

A similar incident on July 2, 2017 caused the train to be late by ninety minutes owing to lack of pushing power and frequent halts en route.

On Nov. 6, 2017, the journey to the hills turned out to be a nightmare as the train halted mid-forest near Hillgrove owing to a valve snag. Technicians from Coonoor were rushed to the spot to repair the fault, causing a delay of four hours.

On December 10, 2017, tourists who booked their journey from Mettupalayam to Coonoor were a disappointed lot after the service was cancelled as its engine, which had developed a technical snag on the previous day was sent for repairs. The train had not returned to Mettupalayam from Coonoor as scheduled after the engine boiler burst on its way to Coonoor. More than 200 passengers were stranded for several hours due to this incident near Hillgrove. On December 9, 2017, shortly after the engine refilled water and the train left Hillgrove, while passing over a bridge, a lead plug of the engine that protects the boiler snapped. The boiler subsequently squirted boiling water and steam causing the engine crew Boopathy, 33, Sathish, 31 and Vinodh, 27, to suffer burn injuries. The train was halted immediately with two coaches stranded on the bridge. The passengers in other two coaches got down and managed to travel by road with the help of some commuters after a trek via a path through the forest to the ghat road way below the hillside. The passengers in other two carriages could neither get down nor travel till a relief engine arrived from Coonoor to haul the train. The train was scheduled to reach Coonoor at 10:30 A.M, suffered a delay of five hours. Consequently the service from Coonoor to Mettupalayam was cancelled and the faulty engine was sent for repair on the following day, resulting in the cancellation of the train service on Sunday Dec. 10, 2017 also. "So, we cancelled the train on Sunday and it may remain cancelled on Monday as well," said a railway official.

The four new engines built at Tiruchirapally between 2011 and 2014 were in the news in recent times for their poor haulage capacity. Hpwever, the steam engine involved in the latest incident was the vintage Swiss-built X-37391 which was completely refurbished in December 2015. NMR enthusiasts opine that it was up to the railway administration to provide a hitch-free service, but it is apparent that this railway is not on the priority list of Railways; and the service is far below global standards despite its World Heritage Site status. A Southern Railway official said that they are concerned about the safety of the passengers.

Ever since this railway was inscribed as a UNESCO World Heritage site in 2005, it has gained popularity. More tourists now visit the region from abroad and from within India, just to experience the 'magical journey' on this unique rack-and-pinion mountain railway – the only one in Asia.

Today, this scenic metre gauge rack railway has some stations lying in a decrepit state. The gangmens' quarters beside the track and cottages for station masters fell into disuse, and forest vegetation took over the abandoned structures. Tracks for crossing trains were uprooted and the stations were shut down. Goods sheds at military stations of Wellington and Aravankadu were closed and tracks were removed; and the vast yard at Ooty is now a grass-land. Despite a surge in revenue of the railway department, this mountain line appears to be on an odyssey to oblivion. "Being a World Heritage site has not helped NMR in any way" feel many rail enthusiasts, "because just a single train service runs to Ooty from Mettupalayam and that too with our continued efforts to prod the railway administration to keep it running daily! Left to Indian Railways it will run erratically, citing a variety of reasons." As Nilgiris Cultural Association president P.S. Sundar said, "The aam admi (common man) in the Nilgiris and those in the State/Centre never bothered about the downslide in the operations of NMR. I don't think they even felt the sound of the loco traversing the hills. Some of them may have looked at the passing by train without a feeling that the train belonged to the Nilgiris."

## Railways Training Institute Proposed at Ooty

In mid January 2018, eathmovers were spotted working in the now vacant yard at Udagamandalam railway station. It is reported to be an ongoing work to construct a Railways Training Institute. Another development was a press report stating that A.K. Kathpal, Principal Chief Mechanical Engineer, Southern Railway, said that wide-ranging measures, including introduction of additional oil-fired locomotives and newly designed coaches are to be introduced on Nilgiri Railway; and these could lead to an increase in the frequency of the trains and also fewer mechanical faults along the rack railway line. Also, two knowledge centres for steam engines were being created, and retired steam personnel in Chennai and Tiruchirapally were being identified. A framework was being created for the knowledge they possess on steam locomotives to be preserved and passed on. Officials added that the NMR heritage coaches were being given a fresh look, while it was expected that there would be Rolling Stock Programme sanction for four additional oil-fired steam engines this year.

It is observed that few people aboard a train on the Nilgiri Mountain Railway seek creature comforts, and they travel to experience and understand how the engineering skills of the bygone era had been harnessed to counter the challenges of constructing a railway over steep mountainous terrain without using modern equipment that is available today. For some it is an accent on nostalgia and a flashback to the pleasures of the past, as they closely observe the quaintness of the trains, engines, signaling and track equipment, and the stations en route. A majority among the younger generation today may have never seen a steam engine in action, because steam traction was phased out well over a decade ago and trains are hauled by diesel or electric locomotives across the country. It is pertinent to note that even though railway officials take cognizance of public demonstrations held to prod them to improve the lot of the Nilgiri Mountain Railway, the fact is that we first need others to appreciate something that we take for granted; and only then do we wake up to realize that the subject is indeed beautiful and needs to be preserved.

The UNESCO inscription states:

**UNESCO, in 2005, has inscribed The Nilgiri Mountain Railway as a World Heritage site, as part of "Mountain Railways of India" since:-**

They are outstanding examples of interchange of values on developments in technology, and the impact of innovative transportation system of the social and economic development of a multicultural region, which was to serve as a model for similar developments in many parts of the world.

The development of railways in the 19th century had a profound influence on social and economic developments in many parts of the world. They are outstanding examples of a technological ensemble, representing different phases of the development in high mountain areas.

*This confirms its exceptional and universal value*
*which requires protection for the benefit of all humanity.*

# Letters That Speak...and Excerpts from Newspapers

## From The Mail, Madras, Jan. 8, 1968

### Ooty Rail Link

While hoping that the Railway authorities will pay heed to Mr. Abraham Paul's views on the proposed dismantling of the Ooty railway line (The Mail, Jan. 5–6), I would like to give some suggestions for the improvement of the railways and prevent the shutdown of this link.

If financial situation and natural barriers are likely to hinder electrification of the railway line to Ooty, there is scope for improving the existing services by making them more comfortable. The carriages can be modernised by having huge plastic windows to offer the traveller a grand view of the scenic panorama of the Nilgiris, thus making the train resemble the viewing cars of the Canadian Pacific Railways.

Buses cover the distance of 22 miles between Mettupalayam and Coonoor in an hour and a half while the train takes almost three hours. Speed and efficiency can be achieved only if the existing line is electrified and suitable locomotives obtained. Swiss Railways now have trains operating on inclines of 30 degrees with ease.

Nevertheless this railway is of great importance and it should be retained and suitable modifications made in the coaches. Electrification of this section of the Southern Railway will be most welcome. Ooty can thus boast of having an ultramodern railway, and this will definitely give a big boost to tourism.

– V.M.G. CHETTUR,
Madras

## A Letter from Ministry of Railways (Railway Board) dated Jan. 18, 1969:

No. TCR/2008/68/Rep/Ooty.

Shri V.M.Govind Chettur, B.Sc.,

Bishop Heber Hall,

Madras Christian College,

Tambaram, Madras-59

Dear Sir,

Sub: Mettupalayam – Ootacamund Line.

With reference to your letter dated 21.12.68 addressed to the Minister for Railways, I am directed to state that no final decision in regard to the closure of Mettupalayam-Ootacamund Line has been taken. I am directed to assure you that all relevant factors will be taken into account before a final decision is taken in regard to closure of this line.

Yours faithfully,
– S.V. Ramasuban
For Secretary, Railway Board.

## From The Indian Express, Mar. 13, 1974

### Ooty Railway

Now that the Government of Madras has urged the retention of the Ooty rail line, and that the railways intend manufacturing metre gauge diesel locomotives for use on hill-railways, it is hoped that speedy dieselisation, or, better, electrification of the Nilgiri railway will be undertaken. This is sure to make this railway really popular and remunerative.

– V.M.G. CHETTUR,
Tambaram

## From The Hindu, Madras, Mar. 13, 1974

### Nilgiri Ghat Railway

The reasons for the Railway's inability to run at least one passenger train a day between Ooty and Mettupalayam and vice versa for the past three months are known to all concerned. The "season" in this so-called Queen of Hill Stations is fast approaching and there appear to be no signs even now to restore even normal services. The local inhabitants have suffered enough. A prompt and assured service is a 'must' throughout the year for this place.

– S.V. KRISHNAN,
Coonoor

## Excerpts from a reply by The Ministry of Railways, New Delhi, on Jan 2, 1972

### Nilgiri Railway – Electrification and Dieselisation

Electrification requires very large initial investments and is justified normally on sections carrying very high densities of traffic. Way and means position regarding funds and foreign exchange being limited, all electrification projects are examined in detail for their financial viability. As per current policy, electrification of trunk routes has to be considered first, followed by isolated sections where financial/economic advantages are substantial. Accordingly, electrification of Nilgiri Hill Railway for the present is not justified.

The dieselisation of Nilgiri Mountain Railway has also been examined but was not found to be economical. The existing steam locos operating on the section are considered to be in a satisfactory condition and do not require replacement.

– V.P. SAWHNEY, Secretary,
Railway Board

## From The Hindu, Madras, Mar. 9, 1972

### "Uneconomic Railway Lines"

The General Manager of the Southern Railway has announced that the Railways would run passenger buses on half a dozen routes over which the existing rail services are considered "uneconomic," and charge normal bus fares in place of the higher rail fares. If the intention is that the Railway would run its own bus service departmentally, in competition with the existing private operators or the State Transport department, there could be nothing wrong in that proposal. But before doing so, there are two aspects to be taken into consideration.

It should be found out whether an "uneconomic" line could be made "economic" by adopting certain measures of operational efficiency and introducing essential passenger amenities. The Nilgiri Hills railway may be taken as a case in point. According to the Railway Board, the loss incurred on this sector varies annually between Rs. 23 and Rs. 26 lakhs. This railway built by Swiss engineers in the late Nineties, and regarded as one of the best tourist attractions in Southern India has seen no improvements in the last sixty years. The type of traction, the speed of the trains, and the level of passenger amenities remain exactly the same as in 1910. Trains still crawl at 8 miles an hour for most of the 29 miles, and takes four hours to reach Ootacamund, whereas a passenger bus does the same distance in half that time. The locos are incapable of hauling more than five coaches, and suffer frequent breakdowns. The fares charged are fantastically high. A first class rail ticket costs Rs. 13, whereas a seat in the first class bus costs just Rs. 4. Only two trains are run daily in each direction. No wonder it is not possible to run the service economically under such conditions!

To improve the usefulness and popularity of this line and to increase the earnings adequately, the Tamil Nadu Railway Users' Chamber recently made the following suggestions to the Union Ministry of Railways: 1) The old "Puffing Billys" should be withdrawn and in their place electric traction, or at least diesel traction, should be introduced, so that more carriages could be attached and the trains speeded up. This would permit a reduction in fares. 2) The "first class" service on these trains is a total waste during the "off-season" (June to February). Even the few passengers who travel are generally free-pass holders. Therefore, during the off season of nine months, second class fares may be charged for first class accommodation, bringing down the fare almost on a par with bus fare. 3) The carriages should be remodeled to provide for some bathrooms and w/c, without which no tourist would like to use the trains. After making on-the-spot enquiries, we are convinced that this uneconomic line could be rendered economic by adopting the suggestions given above.

The other aspect is in regard to the movement of goods. Most of the "uneconomic" lines carry heavy goods and they have to continue to perform this important service even after the passenger traffic has been withdrawn. But the need for these lines may be questioned after some years on the ground that they serve only goods traffic and not the passenger traffic. The TN Railway Users' Chamber would therefore appeal to the Southern Railway to examine ways and means of providing a better and more efficient level of service for passenger trains on the 'uneconomic lines' and try to make them 'economic' before deciding to cancel the trains, and carry the passengers by buses.

– P.S. SUBRAMANIAM, President,<br>
Tamil Nadu Railway Users' Chamber, Madras

## From The Hindustan Times, New Delhi, Nov. 18, 1973

### Train to Ooty

*I,-Divakaran writes from Bangalore:*

A couplet painted on the rocks on the way from Mettupalayam to Ootacamund says:

> *So many people come and go,*
>
> *But the train brings more and more.*

Will they? For how long?

The locomotive that pushes the four-wagon train for 46 km at a speed of 11 km an hour carries a plaque saying that it was made at Winterthur,

Switzerland, in 1920. The firm has stopped production of these engines and spares are not available nor are fresh supplies. The old engine has lost much of its pushing (not pulling) power and the four other engines in service are equally old, it is said. Engineers from Chittaranjan inspected the line some time ago and threw up their hands: they advised against production of such engines. This railway line faces closure the moment these engines stop.

Just as the stage-coach in the West gave place to steam engine the railway here will yield place to the bus. The bus journey is slightly costlier and faster, and travellers will see the beautiful Nilgiris for less time: the flame of the forest in bloom, pines, bamboos and a variety of flowers that will make an exotic bouquet.

Mr. Kalimuthu, brakesman on the train for 22 years, will be the saddest man, for he has enjoyed every minute he spent on the train. The house of the station master at Adderley is named "Vanavasam," and one hopes he enjoyed his forest life too. The British started work on this line in 1886 and completed it 37 years later. We scrap it in much less time. The Swiss have electric trains to serve Alpine towns and their two-wagon-trains carry fewer passengers than one sees on the Ootacamund line.

– Square

## From The Hindustan Times, New Delhi, Dec. 2, 1973

### Train to Ooty

Square's write up on the train to Ooty has saddened many train lovers especially those who have traversed in the scenic Nilgiri Mountain Railway. This railway is a unique piece of engineering skill and the metre gauge line uses a central rack railway on the gradient of 1 in 12.50

between Kallar and Coonoor. No rack exists on the less steep 1 in 25 gradient between Coonoor and Ooty. The line passes through the most scenic part of the Nilgiris providing a leisurely and enjoyable journey to a height of 7,300 ft.

The Railway Ministry should strive to retain and improve this magnificent railway laid by Swiss engineers over 75 years ago during the British regime. If our engineers are unable to improve the line with modern technology and equipment, the Railway Board should seek the help of Swiss engineers as another such rack-railway exists in Switzerland. On-the-spot inquiries prove that this line can be saved by electrification or dieselisation as in the Swiss Alpine railways. In India, the Kalka - Simla narrow gauge line has had diesel traction all the way up the hill since 1971.

If modernised, the Nilgiri Railway will give a big boost to tourism and the economy of the region. Every effort must be made in this direction. On no account should this railway be scrapped.

– V.M.G. CHETTUR,
15, Sunder Nagar, New Delhi

## From The Hindu, Madras, May 1, 1974

### Ooty Then and Now

The decision to scrap this train service between Mettupalayam and Ootacamund is catastrophic. At a time when the Indian economy is cracking under the skyrocketing imported oil prices, it is distressing to learn that the Railway Ministry has done away with the cheaper, coal-based mode of transportation. Instead of conserving costly petroleum this decision is forcing its use. And what will follow if oil imports are slashed to keep the economy from collapsing?

Although the railway route concerned is only about 32 miles in distance, it provided an important and popular mode of transport for commuters, tourists and for materials to and from such vital institutions as the Cordite Factory in Aruvankadu, the Madras Regimental Centre and the Defence Services Staff College, Wellington, not to mention various important industries and agricultural centres in the district.

Costing several crores of rupees, the route is recognised even in this country (U.S.) as a feat of engineering skill and one of the most picturesque anywhere. Furthermore it is providing employment to hundreds in the area. Even if this route was operating at a loss – like most other routes in the country – I am not convinced that the loss generated by this mere 32-mile section stands in the way of any of the advantages outlined.

Instead of abandoning this vital route at this time, the Government should use it to its fullest advantage and help take some of the heat off the worsening oil crisis.

Possibly, a year or two hence, the Government will realise that the route should be reopened, but then give up the idea because it will be too costly to revive.

– VINOD CHHABRA,
Albany, New York

### Excerpts from another letter from The Hindu, May 1, 1974

#### Ooty Then and Now

Much of the natural beauty of Ootacamund as a hill station is a thing of the past. Heavily wooded areas in and around Ooty had shed their verdure and have come under the plough. The peaks and the slopes of the hills stand bereft of trees and green coverage. Buildings, small and big, several of them huts and hovels, have come into existence in the very heart of the town. Due to extensive denudation, rainfall has diminished considerably, and the climate is not what it used to be in the past. The rates in hotels and in the government Tourists' Bungalow are very high and far beyond the reach of middle class tourists, let alone the low income group. The majority of the visitors are those who come by bus and return before dusk.

There is no train service between Mettupalayam and Ootacamund on the Nilgiri Mountain Railway for the past six months. Train journey by the hill railway used to be great fun for the tourists.

Much has to be done to restore the former reputation of this Queen of Hill Stations though top officials and visiting dignitaries do not fail to promise now and then to make this tourist centre more attractive, enjoyable and accessible to all classes of visitors.

– S. RAMABHADRAN,
Ooty

## A news report in The Statesman, New Delhi, Jun. 2, 1976

### Reprieve for a Dream Railway

Coimbatore: The picturesque Nilagiri Mountain Railway – connecting Mettupalayam, the terminus of the broad gauge system of the Southern Railway, in the plains, with the Queen of Hill Stations, Ootacamund, 46 km away at an altitude of 7,500 ft – which has from time to time been threatened with closure, appears to have had a reprieve. Whether that reprieve will be permanent few can say. That will depend upon the extent to which the line is able to recapture its lost traffic and economic viability.

Right now, the line is incurring an annual loss of about Rs. 12 lakh. Southern Railway officials are working hard to wipe out that loss and make the line viable. Meanwhile, as far as one can check, the Railway Board has no intention of closing down the line – although it was a past Chairman of the Board, who, four years ago set off a scare by speaking here of the need for a "hard look" at the line's operational and replacement costs.

The Nilagiri Mountain Railway – opened in 1899 and extended up to Ooty nine years later – is the only hill railway in the world to run round the year. The rest discontinue in winter. Its rack-wheel traction – which keeps the train from slipping on the steep gradients, and which makes the engine not run so much as climb up a kind of ladder – is also unique, in that it survives only here. The line passes through what are probably the the most picturesque hills in the South, along a serpentine course, with several sharp bends, most of them with a curvature of 17 ½ degrees. Its gradients are often as steep as 1 in 12.50. It passes through 16 tunnels and along several girder bridges constructed over deep, precipitous ravines, all of which make the journey to Ooty a memorable experience, filled with gasps of admiration from passengers, as much at the engineering marvel that the line is as at the fairy tale verdure all around. To many in the South this is a "dream railway". Its difficulties, and losses, however, lie in the fact that times have changed, good roads have come up in the area and the average visitor to the hills is in a hurry to get there in a bus that is all ready to whisk him up in about half the time the train takes: in 135 minutes, against the train's running time of 260 minutes. The line's offer of a concessional fare has not made much difference. The line has, besides lost most of its customary freight traffic to lorry-operators who offer several incentives to consignors.

In moments of candour, railway officials confess that, "we are just not used to running this line on a commercial and competitive basis" – although quickly adding that "with some effort, we can certainly make it viable." That effort seems to be on, and officials are said to be earnestly engaged in coaxing back the line's lost traffic.

The line's engines are old: the latest of its 11 engines is 25 years old, and they are subject to frequent failures. "Unless we get new engines, we cannot enhance the frequency of our service, nor can we hope for increased traffic," officials note. Even diesel traction is possible on this line. Only, it would require the strengthening of the culverts and the redoing of the tunnels – at a cost, according to an expert study by the Railway Board eight years ago, of Rs. 2.5 crores at least. After that study, the Board apparently shelved the idea altogether. The public is palpably fond of this dream railway. It is amazing, say many, that officialdom should at all consider dismantling what would be considered a proud national asset and first class tourist attraction anywhere else in the world.

### From The Hindu, Madras, Dec. 6, 1977

## Ooty – Mettupalayam Railway Line

The railway line from Mettupalayam to Ootacamund is a narrow line section. The distance between these two places is about 50 km. The track runs more or less on plains up to Kallar, a place which is about 6 km from Mettupalayam. The train running on this narrow gauge line takes more than 3 ½ hrs to reach Ootacamund from Mettupalayam. The running time of this train can be reduced considerably if tunnels are carved on the ghat just as in the Pune - Bombay line and tunnel railway is introduced in this section. Ootacamund is a tourist centre attracting tourists from various parts of India and even from foreign countries. At present, most of the passengers who are going to Ooty travel by road, because of the prolonged duration of this railway journey. If the railway introduces tunnel railway it will not only increase the passengers by rail thereby increasing the revenue, but it will provide an opportunity for the tourists to see the panoramic valleys of this Blue Mountain and enjoy the natural beauty. During rainy season the track is blocked by heavy boulders due to earth slips. This problem also could be overcome by introducing tunnel railway. The railway authorities should examine the feasibility of a tunnel railway line in this section which would be welcomed by one and all.

– I.R. LOGANATHAN,
Madras

## From The Hindu, Madras, Dec. 13, 1977

### Mettupalayam – Ootacamund Line

The Nilagiri Mountain Railway is a metre-gauge line and is a "tunnel railway" as the line has 16 tunnels between Kallar and Ooty on the ghat section. The scenic journey is rather time consuming due to the vintage steam locomotives built in 1920 by the Swiss Locomotive Works, Winterthur. What is now required to speed up the trains on this picturesque railway is electric traction or diesel traction to start with. For example, small trains of two-car units can be operated at 30 minute intervals, instead of the six-coach steam train. By this way, the journey of 28 ½ miles between Mettupalayam and Ooty can easily be done in a hour and a half instead of the present three and a half hour trip. With the present expertise available, the Railways would be able to modernise the line.

– V.M. GOVIND KRISHNAN,
New Delhi

## From The Indian Express, Madurai, Jun. 30, 1978

### Nilgiri Railway

It is time the Railway Ministry seriously considered dieselisation or electrification of the popular Nilgiri Mountain Railway. There are just two pairs of trains each way now between Mettupalayam and Ooty, the Queen of Hill Stations. This is highly inadequate.

I found the coaches carrying about 120 passengers each in a jam-packed state (whereas a coach is meant to seat only 56 in comfort). This overloading results in breakdown of the trains on the steep ascent between Kallar and Coonoor and can be avoided if more trains could be run. This can easily be achieved with electrification, for trains could be run at hourly intervals or less, and it is much cheaper to operate than the present vintage steam locos.

Being a great tourist attraction and the only mountain railway in India with the rack-system, this metre-gauge railway deserves better treatment. The narrow-gauge rail line to Simla has been having diesel traction since 1971, but the journey there is not half as scenic as on the Nilgiri Railway.

A concrete effort on the part of the Railway Ministry is called for to improve the lot of this dream railway.

– V.M.G. KRISHNAN,
New Delhi

## A news report in The Indian Express, Madurai, Dec. 4, 1977

### Ooty Line Cleared, But No Coal for Trains

Ootacamund, Dec. 3: The land slips on the Nilgiri mountain railway from Mettupalayam to Ootacamund has been cleared, but the train service could not be restored for want of coal, the District Collector, Mr. Inbasagaran told newsmen here today.

## From The Indian Express, July 13, 1979

### Nilgiri Railway in Bad Shape

The Nilgiri mountain railway linking Ootacamund, the queen of hill stations, with the plains of Coimbatore district, is now in a very bad shape and may soon become extinct by slow wear and tear and sheer neglect. This is not the fault of Southern Railway authorities. The fault is entirely with the Ministry of Railways which has failed to recognise the worth and importance of this hill railway and has taken no steps whatever to keep it in an efficient and going condition.

The Swiss engineers, who built this super-engineering marvel in the last century, would stand aghast if they were to witness its condition today.

The 75-year-old "Puffing Billies" used on these trains, have reached the end of their life but nobody has cared to replace them. The old passenger coaches with narrow benches and no toilet facilities, groan, and creak even when traveling at the ridiculously low speed of 10 km per hour, and nobody has thought of replacing them.

The time taken for the 46 km journey between Ootacamund and Mettupalayam increase with each revision of the time-table because of the steady deterioration in the condition of the track, engines and coaches. The so-called Nilgiri Express train now takes five hours to cover the distance, whereas some ten years ago the time taken was only 4 ½ hrs. This is an indication of the rot that has set in.

The absurdly high fare by train is by calculating not on the actual mileage basis but on "inflated mileage," which works out to 2 ½ times the normal fare. This antiquated system could have been tolerated in pre independent India when only the white rulers and rich Indians were expected to "patronise" the hills, but now these hills are visited by thousands of Indians of moderate means. If the fares were placed reasonably on par with the bus fares it is certain that the Nilgiri mountain railway will become immensely popular and there will be a large shift of passengers from road to the rail.

The reason for this neglect, it is said, is that it has been classified as an "uneconomic railway". But has anyone taken the trouble to find out why it is so and whether it can be made "economic"? It is high time that the Ministry of Railways woke up to these needs and introduced some effective measures for changing this "uneconomic" line into a "economic" one and prevent this popular railway from "dying a natural death."

– R.S. SUBRAMANIAN,
Madras

## From The Indian Express, July 26, 1979

### Nilgiris Railway

When all over the world, the Governments are boosting their tourist trade by developing their rail communications by enlightened transport policies. For us in India, and Tamilnadu in particular, to neglect the Nilgiris Railway, and allow it to "die a natural death," (as mentioned by R.S. Subramaniam – July 13) is a tragic step, which the Ministry of Tourism should thwart, if necessary, in conjunction with the Ministry of Commerce.

– A.C. NATARAJAN,
Tenkasi

## From The Indian Express, Madurai, Aug. 4, 1981

### Ooty Rail Line

It is highly regrettable that the Railway Board is considering scrapping of the Nilgiris railway line. The reason seems to be that the section is uneconomical. If one carefully looks at the problem it will be evident that the reason for this lies with the Railways themselves. Since laying this line in 1897 or so the Railways have not effected any improvement or modernisation. While the running time from Mettupalayam to Coonoor by road has improved from 2 ½ hours at the beginning of the century to 1 ¼ hours now, the time taken by train has remained a poor 2 ½ hours from the date of inception. So you cannot blame the public. Besides, the Railways run only two services and that too with two II class carriages and so the people have no other go except to travel by road. Even then most of the women prefer to travel only by train.

When the Railways boast of running superfast express trains like Tamilnadu, Vaigai and Kovai, it is a sad reading that they cannot modernise this wonderful railway line and choose to scrap it. Over the years, so much of improvement in traction has been achieved that modernisation like electrification of 20-km route can solve the problem or what is called "Dwarf Shunt Vehicle" can be produced and operated.

I request the Government of Tamilnadu and the Tourist Department to prevail upon the Central Government to improve the efficiency of the only hill railway in the South.

– DR. B. SUDARSANAM,
Coonoor

## From The Statesman, New Delhi, Nov. 7, 1981

### 100 Years After

It was interesting to read in "100 years ago" (October 27–28) news about the construction of the Nilgiri Railway, which was opened to traffic in June 1899 between Mettupalayam and Coonoor and extended to Ootacamund in 1908.

The vintage steam engines built by the Swiss Locomotive Works, Winterthur, have long passed the prime of their lives, and the trains which used to comprise six coaches now run with three. The resulting confusion, due to lack of accommodation puts off the traveller. The trains break down frequently at Kallar where the ascent begins as the engines have lost their pushing power.

Several representations to the Ministry of Railways have been futile and no attempt has been made to improve this unique mountain railway. With each revision of the time-table, the running time uphill between Mettupalayam and Ooty has been increasing; it was 3 hours 55 minutes in April 1966 and is 4 hours and 40 minutes in April 1981. There were four pairs of passenger trains on the 46-kilometre-long route, now there is just one pair.

Official indifference should not be allowed to impede modernisation of this mountain railway. With present day technology, suitable electric engines can be obtained to run this railway and the coaches should be remodelled to offer the travellers a grand view of the panorama of the Nilgiris.

– V.M. GOVIND KRISHNAN,
New Delhi

## From The Hindu, Madras, Mar. 3, 1982

### Nilgiris Mountain Railway

The gruesome train accident on the Nilgiris railway should prove to be an eye-opener, for official indifference over the years has turned a blind eye to several constructive and meaningful suggestions by the public and the Tamil Nadu Government to modernise this unique and picturesque mountain railway. The Centre chose to allow a mishap to occur before thinking over the issue.

It is well known that the vintage Swiss-built steam locos (some over 50 years old) have lost their efficiency, the mountain track and rack-rails need replacement, and the rolling stock need overhauling; but these urgent needs are shelved in the name of economy and to provide a case for uneconomic operation of the line and allow it to die.

It is hoped that the Railway Ministry would now seriously consider modernising the line by electric traction as this would be more economical and also provide a boost to tourism in the region. It would not be out of place to mention that the narrow gauge Kalka – Simla line has had diesel traction since 1971, whereas the metre-gauge Nilgiri mountain railway has seen practically no improvement since its opening in June 1899.

– V.M. GOVIND KRISHNAN,
New Delhi

From The Hindu, Madras, Mar. 3, 1982

## Nilgiris Mountain Railway

The Nilgiri railway accident, involving a goods train carrying precious coal to the hills is a sad reflection, in general, of the inefficiency of the railway maintenance programme over the years, and the failure to adopt necessary safety measures for safeguarding the property and precious lives of people.

The unfortunate brake-man and the fireman of the engine of the goods train seem to have shouted "The brakes have failed only God can save us." The unique rack and pinion system of the mountain track which has given satisfactory service all these years seems to have failed. Is it because on account of wear and tear of the rack and pinion over the years which has not been replaced whenever found necessary?

The railway authorities must take steps to improve the line for giving better service by electrifying the traction from Mettupalayam to Ooty and also providing high powered electric engines and at the same time examine the question of realignment of the railway line wherever possible and necessary.

The question of changing from the metre gauge to broad gauge for this section or at least run it on the standard gauge of 4 ft. 8 inches must be considered. The extension of the railway line from Ooty to the Hindustan Film Company and also up to Naduvattam and other places may be considered.

– R. SANKARAN,
Coimbatore

## From Indian Express, New Delhi, Oct. 22, 1982

### Nilgiri Railway

The Mettupalayam-Ooty rail service, suspended from February 21, following the first ever mishap on the mountain railway, was resumed from October 2 after a break of seven months. In the Madurai edition of Indian Express dated April 29 it was reported that diesel traction was to be introduced in two months time. No further progress seems to have been made, and the solitary through passenger train to Ooty continues to be pushed uphill by a 1920 vintage Swiss steam engine. Modernisation of this meter-gauge mountain railway is essential.

– V.M. GOVIND KRISHNAN,
A31/496, Air-India Colony,
New Delhi-110057

## A news report item in The Hindu, Madras, Jan, 22, 1986

### Railway Station Master Found Dead

Udhagamandalam, Jan. 21: Mr. P.V. Gopinathan Unni (42), local Railway Station Master was found dead in a pit at the railway yard here on Monday night with injuries on the neck. A police dog arrived here from Coimbatore to help in the investigations.

## From Indian Express, Madurai, June 23, 1986

### Nilgiri Rail Link

Almost the whole of Southern Railway has been dieselized and steam traction phased out, except on the scenic mountain railway to Ooty where vintage Swiss-built metre gauge steam engines are still in use.

Despite much talk, since 1982, about the proposed speedy induction of diesel engines specially made for the rack and pinion traction between Kallar and Coonoor, nothing worthwhile has been done in this direction till today. Will the Southern Railway authorities ensure modernisation of this 46 km. line as soon as possible?

– GOVIND KRISHNAN,
Mt. Pleasant, Coonoor-2

## Excerpts from an article in The Statesman, New Delhi, Dec. 21, 1985

### The Changing Face of Ooty

The rail journey up from Mettupalayam, though not the speediest, remains one of the great steam experiences still left in the world. The steep climb to Ooty is only 46 km by rail and the buses do it in less than half the time. But once you get aboard the smart blue and white liveried rake, pushed by the famous extra-pistoned tankers, you will exult in the lost glory of the steam engine, as she charges up the steep gradients with thunderous pantings, locked on to a central third rail to assist the great-hearted locomotive.

This metre-gauge line was the pride of railway engineering when it was constructed more than a hundred years ago. The development of the valley followed the railway line and in Coonoor, the solid stone railway station, built in 1893, still marks the centre of the town, and all traffic comes to a standstill when the train appears. Nowadays that means only twice a day. The loco sheds in Coonoor maintain a dozen of these tankers and it is a tribute to the workmen that after all the terrific pressure these locomotives come under on these merciless gradients, most of them are still fighting fit.

– BILL AITKEN

## Excerpts from a letter in Indian Express, New Delhi, Sep. 21, 1986

### The Honeymoon is Over

Denudation of the dense tropical jungle has played havoc with the climate of the entire Nilgiri range. At Coonoor, summer temperatures now touch almost 30 deg. C and one sweat profusely after a short walk. Refrigerators are being increasingly used in homes, out of sheer necessity, and the time is not far off when ceiling fans will be seen too. Rainfall is negligible and the water crisis is an everyday affair. It is high time a stop was put to this thoughtless deforestation in the name of development.

The winding ghat road from Mettupalayam in the plains is choked with vehicular traffic, and this has further increased with the total suspension of freight traffic by rail since 1982, following the first ever mishap on the 90-year old mountain railway when a freight train plunged into a ravine. Now, a solitary passenger train is run from Mettupalayam to Ooty and back to connect the train from Madras. The carriages have been reduced from six to four or three, despite the rush in passenger traffic. This is because of the dilapidated state of the vintage Swiss steam engines on this route. Official indifference seems to have come in the way of improving this vital rail link.

The Tamil Nadu government and those in power at the Centre should see that no further deforestation occurs anywhere in the Nilgiris and the

Western Ghats in general. All further projects involving felling of trees in the name of development must be shelved, and existing facilities should be improved, such as the augmentation of water supply, resurfacing potholed roads, massive afforestation, and the dieselisation of the scenic mountain railway to Ooty.

– GOVIND KRISHNAN,
New Delhi

## From Indian Express, Madurai, June 18, 1987

### Nilgiri Railway

I had the occasion of traveling by the unique metre-gauge rack railway from Mettupalayam to Coonoor in the Nilgiris after a decade. I was shocked to see the dilapidated state of the vintage coaches (built in 1914) and the poorly maintained track and stations en route notably Adderley and Runneymede. The scarred landscape of the once evergreen mountains was a pathetic sight. The undergrowth has vanished, the forests are dry, and forest fires have laid bare huge patches of jungle. No more can one experience the sights of gushing streams, waterfalls, dripping moss-filled rocks etc en route. This is the effect of deforestation and unplanned development in the Nilgiris.

The present Minister of State for Railways has introduced diesel traction in the narrow gauge lines in the Gwalior area and in the Neral - Matheran line in Maharashtra. "No funds," or "not profitable" is the stock reply when it comes to the modernisation of Nilgiri Railway, showing official indifference.

What should be done is 1) the coaches should be built anew with lighter material, huge windows to enjoy the scenery and the provision of toilets in trains is also required, 2) the track should be properly maintained and electrified, since the Swiss who built this line and the engines, have now electrified mountain railways. Besides, electric traction is the most economical and efficient means of railway transport.

– V.M. GOVIND KRISHNAN,
Coonoor

## From the Indian Express, Madurai, June 29, 1988

### Mountain Train

The unique rack and pinion system metre-gauge mountain railway between Mettupalayam and Ooty continues to be in a state of neglect. Most of the vintage Swiss-made steam engines are unfit for the steep gradient of 1 in 12.50 ft on the ghat section between Kallar and Coonoor, and freight traffic on the line was suspended since 1982. No effort has been initiated to modernise the 46-km line by electric traction (which incidentally is more economical and efficient). The ancient rolling stock should be replaced by new coaches with large windows, and with toilet facility in the carriages (as on the neat and clean diesel engine-hauled narrow gauge railway from Kalka to Simla in Himachal Pradesh). Suitable electric engines could be imported for the purpose and the scenic mountain railway should be modernised soon with electric traction and not allowed to rot away.

– GOVIND KRISHNAN,
Coonoor (Nilgiris)

From The Hindu, New Delhi, Feb. 28, 1989

## Nilgiri Mountain Railway

The unique metre gauge mountain railway between Mettupalayam and Udhagamandalam continues to be in a state of neglect thanks to official indifference. The vintage rolling stock and the tracks are poorly maintained, and so also the stations en route such as Adderley and Runneymede. A solitary passenger train runs daily offering connection to the Nilgiri Express from Madras Central. This train takes almost five hours to cover the 46 km stretch between the plains and Ooty. It is usually packed to capacity. Yet, as per the Railway Ministry, the line is said to be 'uneconomical', and no effort is made to make it more attractive to travellers. Out of the eight vintage Swiss built steam engines on this line, only four are suitable for the steep 1 in 12.5 ft. gradient between Kallar and Coonoor, and the remaining engines are used only between Coonoor and Ooty where the maximum gradient is 1 in 25 ft and the centrally laid rack-rails are not there on this stretch.

Due to unplanned development of the hills and extensive deforestation, the hills are rather bare, and no more does one enjoy sights of waterfalls, gushing streams, and moss-covered rocks en route. Forest fires have also occurred rather frequently due to the resultant drought.

On April 28, 1982, Mr. Verghese Anver, the then GM of the Southern Railway said that diesel traction would be introduced in two months time on this line. This was repeated by successive GMs, and on Feb. 5, 1986 an item in a New Delhi daily mentioned that the RDSO, Lucknow, was designing a locomotive suited for this stretch. In April 1987, the Railway Board confirmed in writing that there was no likelihood of introducing diesel traction in the near future, on this line.

The present Minister for Railways has introduced diesel engines on the narrow gauge lines around Gwalior, and also in Maharashtra on the

Neral – Matheran line. The Kangra Valley and the Kalka – Simla lines in the Himachal Pradesh have diesel traction for over a decade. "No funds," or "Not profitable," is the stock reply when it comes to the modernisation of the Nilgiri Railway.

What is required to be done now is: 1) the coaches should be built anew with lighter material and huge windows to enjoy the scenery. Besides, toilets should be provided in the carriages (as no toilet facility exists on trains on this line). 2) The track should be properly maintained and electrified, since the Swiss who constructed this line have electric traction on their mountain railways.

With electric traction, more trains with two or four coach units could be run at speeds of 20 to 40 km taking less time to cover the distance, and wean away the traffic from the already congested ghat road. To start with, electric traction could be introduced on the Coonoor – Ooty stretch and later extended to the steep ghat section between Coonoor and Mettupalayam.

Electric traction is the most economical and efficient means of rail transportation.

– V.M. GOVIND KRISHNAN,
New Delhi

## From The Hindu, Madras, Apr. 7, 1989

### Mountain Railway

Apropos of Mr. V.M. Govind Krishnan's letter on the subject (The Hindu, Feb 28) I would like to mention that there is absolutely no excuse for the Railways not modernising the beautiful Nilgiris mountain railway. If the Railways are unable to maintain the line it should either hand it over to the State Government or it could be jointly operated by both the Centre and the State. The line should be electrified or at least special diesel locomotives obtained to run the trains efficiently and faster. The length of the line is, after all, a mere 46 km and it should not be a problem to modernise it with the expertise available. The time to do it is now.

– AMAR SEKHAR,
Madras

## Excerpts from a news report in Indian Express, Madurai, June 11, 1989

### Closure of Nilgiris Railway Ruled Out

Udhagamandalam, June 10: Mr. K.V. Balakrishnan, Member, Railway Board, told Pressmen at Lovedale, near here, on Friday that the Nilgiris mountain railway would not be closed on any account though it was running on loss. Though there was a clamour for dieselising this track, he said that it was not desirable to have a diesel engine because the steam engine was more attractive and people from foreign countries including Australia had come here to see this engine. It was more of a tourist attraction.

When requested to increase the number of trains from Ooty to Mettupalayam as there was only one trip at present, he said, that there was not sufficient passengers.

– FAC

## Excerpts from news report in The Times of India, Bombay, Apr. 19, 1987

### Towards An Industry-Free Nilgiris

"The best industries for Nilgiris is no industry," observed speakers at a seminar to create awareness among people on the ecological imbalance arising out of large-scale degradation of forests and industrial pollution in the Nilgiris, one of the oldest geological formation.

It was time for action to save the Nilgiris from further degradation, they said at the seminar, organised by the "Save Nilgiris campaign," a group of environmental activists striving to arouse public opinion in this regard, reports PTI.

### National Rail Museum, New Delhi – NMR Exhibits displayed

A letter from Ministry of Railways (Railway Board), Rail Bhavan, New Delhi-110001 dated May 8/15, 1991, in response to my letter to the Director, National Rail Museum, about re-locating the out-door exhibits of Nilgiri Railway (NMR) displayed there:

No.90/Museum/Exhibit
Shri Govind Krishnan
B 11/126 Air India Colony,
Vasant Vihar
New Delhi-110057

Sub: Locomotive No. 37385 X (MG) on display in the museum

Many thanks for your letter dt-20.4.91 on the above subject. It is the usual practice in the museum that the exhibits displayed are given its original numbers, colour scheme and livery, and the railway to which it originally belonged. For the information of the visitors a display board is placed by the side of the engine giving the other important technical details including the zonal railway on which it subsequently worked.

In the case of 37385 X (MG) Locomotive it originally belonged to Nilgiri Mountain Railway (N.M.R.), and S.I.R. and S.R. had no domain over it till it was taken over by S.I.R. in 1908 and S. Rly in 1952–53. Your suggestion of keeping the coach along with the engine is being examined as it involves a lot of movement of other stock placed on MG siding.

Thanking you,

Yours faithfully,

– RAM SARAN

Joint Director/Rail Museum

Chanakyapuri, New Delhi-21

### A news report in The Hindu, Madras, Feb. 24, 1992

## Ooty railway station given face lift

Udhagamandalam, Feb. 23

The 84-year old terminal station of the mountain railway line at Udagamandalam is being given a face lift. The main lobby is being widened and separate waiting rooms are being provided for men and women. The work on improving the station is done in phases and there is proposal to provide a lounge for VIPs. The quaint look of the station would be preserved, it was said.

– Our Correspondent

### Excerpts from a news report in Indian Express, Coimbatore, Aug. 25, 1992

## Package tours by Nilgiris Mountain Railway suggested

Coonoor – The Coonoor Citizens Forum has appealed to the General Manager of Southern Railway, Mr. S.H. Babu, to introduce tourism packages in the Nilgiris Mountain Railway.

Mr. S. Rajkumar (President), Dr. Harshavardhan (Jt Secretary) and Chandru Rajbettan (Member) of the forum called on Mr. Babu who visited Coonoor recently.

The delegates of the forum suggested that the NMR re-designed to introduce comfortable coaches. The new coaches will serve for package tour. The frequency of the service has to be increased. The tariff can be fixed high to match the standard of service.

The forum highlighted the need for manufacturing suitably designed diesel locomotives at the earliest. It said that if this was not done within the next 10 years the NMR would cease operation.

Mr. Babu drew the attention of the delegates to the huge loss suffered by the NMR. He urged the tea industry to use the railways to transport tea. He also requested the tea exporters to use the container facility.

### From The Hindu, Madras, June 7, 1993

### Shorn of Grandeur, Not It's Charm

The hooting that reverberated across the sylvan valleys of Ooty, the scenic headquarters of the Nilgiris district, is no longer heard.

The nearly century old steam locomotive that used to haul up and down countless tourists through the enchanting mountain ranges at last bade adieu to the picturesque town of Ooty, with it was gone one of the grandeurs of the British regality symbolized with the queen of hill stations that would certainly be missed by the residents of the town.

A remodelled diesel locomotive took over the proud place of the steam engine to haul passengers in the tourists favoured mountain railway between Coonoor and Udagamandalam stations from April this year.

Despite the railway's dieselisation drive closing in on the famous Nilgiris mountain railway too, all is however not lost for those craving to travel by the steam locomotive as it will continue to operate hauling passengers from Mettupalayam at the foot of the hills to Coonoor atop a section which, with its bewitching age-old "sholas," deep ravines and undulating woods, offers a veritable feast to the travellers.

According to railway sources, the section during 1990–91 could earn only Rs. 94.69 lakhs from passenger traffic, by handling that year about 2.27 lakh passengers, and its net revenue from freight was only Rs. 10.44 lakhs, whereas the railway incurred about Rs. 1.48 crores towards the working expenditure alone for the Mettupalayam – Udagamandalam section without computing the capital depreciation.

The railway authorities feel that though the sector had vast freight potential because of the vital brimming plantation economy in the entire Nilgiris region the railway could not benefit much and the road transport corner all the freights depriving the railways' share due to operational advantages enjoyed by the former.

– V.P.

### From Indian Express, Coimbatore, Jan. 14, 1994

## Ooty Rail Line in Limbo

The metre gauge mountain railway between Mettupalayam and Ooty in the Nilgiris is the only one of its kind in India to run on a rack and pinion system. The recent massive landslide damaged about a furlong length of the track and over a kilometer of the main ghat road. The railway authorities seem to be in no hurry to restore the track, allowing the line to rot into oblivion.

This should not be allowed. Every effort must be made immediately to restore the track and resume trains. Only last year in April, a diesel engine was introduced for the Coonoor – Ooty stretch of the railway, and this service too has been suspended for no ostensible reason.

A suitable diesel engine for the Mettupalayam – Coonoor section must be made available immediately to replace the vintage Swiss-made steam engines on this line, and more services should be operated. The old heavy rolling stock should be replaced by lighter ones.

– V.M. GOVIND KRISHNAN,
New Delhi

## Excerpts from a news item in The Statesman, New Delhi, Oct. 14, 1994

### Old Beauty New Make-Up

Coimbatore, Oct. 13 - The narrow gauge train takes about five hours to cover 45.9 km at an average speed of 13 km per hour. Time consuming and boring? Far from it anyone who has traveled by the Nilgiri Mountain Rail from Mettupalayam to Udagamandalam (Ooty) over the past 95 years will tell you that the steep journey from 330 metres above mean sea level to 2,200 metres above MSL, is really fascinating.

It climbs an average of one metre for every 7.35 m, the steepest being one in about three metres, passing through 208 sharp curves (the sharpest one being of 17.5 degrees) crosses 250 bridges, an average of six for every km and travels through 16 tunnels in an area that gets ceaseless rainfall of 125 cm per annum. Stated way back in 1899, initially between Mettupalayam and Coonoor before being extended to Ooty in 1908, NMR is one of the cherished legacies of the British, reports PTI.

But in patronizing the legacy on popular demand, the Railways are really maintaining a white elephant, according to the Southern Railways' Palakkad Divisional Manager, Mr. S. Dasarathy. The railways are today planning many innovations to meet the demands of the tourists. "In our efforts to continue the service, we are trying to cut down the operational costs and make it a viable proposition," the Divisional Manager says.

The steam locomotives used here were manufactured in Sweden, weighing 48–50 tons with a high steaming capacity producing horse power equal to the one produced by a 220-ton steam engine, he says. The Railways were spending Rs. 2,500 per ton of coal for operating them. In order to cut down the costs, the Railways had experimented with diesel.

### Excerpts from a news report in The Times of India, New Delhi, Aug. 9, 1995

### Indian Locomotives Steam Up Passion

Bombay, Aug. 8 - The Indian Railways' decision to sell nine vintage steam engines has excited considerable interest among international organisations devoted to the preservation of old locomotives, but raised concern among railway enthusiasts here who feel the engines should be conserved within the country.

Indian Railways have announced the sale through advertisements. Each engine will cost local buyers Rs. 750000, while foreigners will have to pay $.25,000. The director of a multinational company in Bombay Jean Francois Andrist, who is also the vice-president of the Switzerland Railway Preservation Society, said he had already conveyed news of the proposed sale to his friends in Europe.

Viraf Mulla, who has converted his house in Borivli into a virtual railway museum said: "This priceless heritage must remain in India. Indian

Railways can certainly preserve the engines by having special runs of trains with these engines which can be a great tourist draw." The steam engine's characteristic smoke, a distinctive rhythm and hoot, and the fireman shoving coal into the red hot flames, is described as "sheer poetry," while "diesel and electric engines are so prosaic, so monotonous, mere box-like structures," says Mukund Matapurkar, an electric engine driver of the Central Railways.

## Request for Commemorative Postage Stamp

A letter dated Dec. 12, 1996 from Government of India, Ministry of Communications, Department of Post, New Delhi, vide their Ref. No. 16–104/96-Phil, in response to my request to have a postage stamp issued to commemorate the Centenary of the Nilgiri Mountain Railway in June 1999:

> Sub: Proposal for issue of stamp on 100 Years of Nilgiri Mountain Railway

Sir,

Kindly refer to your letter dated 31–10–96 on the above subject. Proposals for new stamps are examined in the light of existing guidelines & these are adhered to rigidly. A stamp has already been released on Nilgiri Mountain Railway on 16–4–93. As a matter of policy, this Department does not issue more than one stamp on the same issue. It is therefore not possible to consider this proposal.

Yours faithfully,

– P.D. Tshering

Asstt. Director General (Phil)

**My repartee** dated Dec. 17, 1996 to Asst. D.G. (Phil), Dept. of Post, New Delhi, enclosing photocopies of the stamps issued in 1982 and 1993 on Darjeeling Himalayan Railway:

> Sub: Proposal for issue of stamp on 100 years of Nilgiri Mountain Railway

Sir,

Please refer to your letter no. 16–104/96-Phil dated Dec. 12th 1996, on the above subject.

The stamp depicting a locomotive of the Nilgiri Railway was issued on 16–4–93 as part of a series of stamps on Mountain Locomotives. There were some factual errors in the brochure issued along with the First Day Cover at that time. The said series of stamps also depicted a locomotive of the Darjeeling Himalayan Railway, despite the fact that a stamp was issued in 1982 to commemorate 100 years of D.H.R. Similarly, I had requested for issue of a stamp on 100 yrs of N.M.R, which is an altogether different theme than the one issued earlier on Mountain Locomotives.

So, it is not a question of more than one stamp on the same issue. How else would you explain the numerous stamps issued on Mahatma Gandhi, J.L. Nehru and Indira Gandhi? Are they not monotonously repeated?

In the light of the above, I request you to consider my proposal for a stamp on the Centenary of Nilgiri Mountain Railway.

Yours faithfully,

– V.M. Govind Krishnan

## From Indian Express, Coimbatore, Nov. 4, 1997

### Mountain Train

I am one of the few old residents of this Queen among Hill resorts of India. I have been living here since 1952. As a student I used to visit Ooty by train from Mangalore at a special concession price. This concession was available for all tourists visiting this hill station by train. I used to enjoy this travel.

This Nilgiri Mountain Railway, though nearly 100 years old, has given so much of joy and excitement to the tourists who really want to enjoy leisurely holidays in this cool and pleasant hill station.

I have read the history of this Nilgiri Mountain Railway and I am intensely aware of the fact the people responsible for the completion of this magnificent project, have done a great job. It is considered as a marvel of engineering skill, but, unfortunately, it has remained what it was when launched 100 years ago. No thought has been given as to how this Mountain Railway could be improved, travel made more comfortable, engine replaced with modern diesel engines or electric locomotives and travel made faster and more enjoyable. Same old engines are hauling a few coaches with great difficulties. The passenger coaches have remained the same. I consider it a sad state of affairs.

I am unable to understand why the railway workshops cannot make new locomotives to replace the 100-year-old locomotives of the Nilgiri Mountain Railway. There were proposals to buy five new locomotives from Switzerland at a very high cost of Rs. 20 crores each. I fail to understand why our engineers and our workshops cannot make these locomotives. If so, it is indeed a sad state of affairs.

I consider it a national pride, during this Golden Jubilee year of Independence, to produce and provide our people what our country needs.

I had the privilege of travelling in an electric locomotive in Switzerland and to the top of Swiss Alps. It was such a beautiful train and it was an exciting experience. I feel very sad to find that we in India have such wonderful things. But we don't enrich our life by improving what we have with us.

It is absolutely necessary to improve the Nilgiri Mountain Railway by replacing the 100-year-old engines and 100-year-old coaches and attract far more tourists to enjoy the breath-taking travel. Otherwise, it will soon have a natural death. Do it before it is too late.

– U. SRIPATHI RAO,
Shree Nivas, 133/A, Peyton Road, Ooty

## From The Sunday Statesman, New Delhi, Feb. 8, 1998

### Neglected Lifeline

The great feat of engineering – the Konkan Railway - has now been fully commissioned, traversing the rugged Western Ghats. It reflects upon the prowess of our engineers and all those who helped in the realisation of the vast project.

However, another marvel of engineering skill of the erstwhile British rule in India – the NMR (Nilgiri Mountain Railway), a 46-km track between Mettupalayam and Ooty, is crying for attention, languishing for months with disrupted service, lack of maintenance and no zeal amongst the zonal railway authorities for maintaining efficient and regular services. This is a far cry from the well-looked after mountain lines in the North such as the Kalka – Simla and the Pathankot – Jogindernagar narrow gauge lines.

The time is now ripe to form a company to improve the line by means of electrification as on its Swiss counterpart, and perhaps to extend it on the northern slopes of the Nilgiris from Ooty to Mysore.

Presently, the proposal to import four new oil-fired steam locos from Switzerland, specialised to operate on the rack and pinion stretch of the railway from Kallar to Coonoor, is still under consideration.

The vintage fleet of coal-fired steam engines made in Switzerland, now in use, has outlived their utility and is prone to breakdowns en route. Due to cannibalisation of parts, the number of "efficient" locomotives has now been reduced from 14 to just three.

It is felt that our own expertise is good enough to manufacture similar engines after a prototype is imported. Now that the railway is in its 100th year of operation, an all-out effort must be made to improve the lot of the N.M.R. Pecuniary considerations should not be a hindrance to its betterment, and the cherished lifeline to the Nilgiris should be improved at all costs.

– GOVIND KRISHNAN,
New Delhi

Former BBC (India) Chief of Bureau, Sir Mark Tully, who travelled by NMR wrote:

"The idyllic way to reach Ooty, from Mettupalayam, is to hop onto the Nilgiri Mountain Railway, one of the world's steepest, fully operational rack and adhesion rail systems. Then commences a 46-km and four-and-half-hour long journey."

Prominent theatre personality, Sunit Tandon wrote, "One of my favourite getaway spots is Ooty. An ideal mode of communication is to take the railroad to Ooty."

## From The New Indian Express, Coimbatore, Feb. 1, 1999

### NMR's Past Glory

I read with interest and amusement the lengthy article about the Nilgiris Mountain Railway (NMR) by S. Gururajan (NIE, Jan 18). Does the NMR really deserve all the hue and cry being made over it for the past many years? Whatever may be its glorious past, there is no denying the fact that today the NMR does not mean much to either the residents of the Nilgiris or tourists.

In this age when everything is moving at break-neck speed very few would knowingly endure a tiresome journey of three hours from Mettupalayam to Coonoor. Even here there is no guarantee that the rail engine will not lose stamina half way through and start huffing and puffing while the passengers literally have their heart in their mouth. After giving its occupants a steam and coal bath when the train finally offloads them in the hill station the refrain is often of disgust and anger. And if some unsuspecting tourists do plan to endure this agony, the train is mercifully off the rails for long periods at a stretch due to frequent blockages en route.

If at all there is any issue in the NMR that deserves attention, it is the issue of facilities (not) provided to passengers. When one buys a ticket at the Coonoor railway station one cannot assume that he has got himself a seat in the train. More often than not he will have to travel standing all the way. There was a time when additional coaches would be attached from Coonoor to accommodate any extra rush but not any more.

What is the purpose of prolonging the life of NMR unless the requisite infrastructure and minimum facilities are first ensured? In its present condition, who needs NMR? Not the people of the Nilgiris, for sure.

– MAHENDRA SETHIA,
Coonoor

## Excerpts from a news report in The Hindu, Coimbatore, Mar. 18, 1999

### Neglect of NMR in centenary year decried

Udhagamandalam, March 17 - Since early this year, the Nilgiris Mountain Railway (NMR) line between Mettupalayam in the plains and Udagamandalam is often being discussed. An oft-repeated question is: "Will it be curtains for the 100-year line?"

This is the centenary year of the NMR which was laid from Mettupalayam to Coonoor, by the Madras Railway Company, a British firm, under an agreement with the then Government of Madras. It was extended to Ootacamund by 1908.

That the centenary of this unique railway line should be celebrated in a big way, in the Nilgiris, is felt by the people. But, they regret that due to neglect and callousness on the part of the authorities, this "marvel of engineering skill," is being made to struggle for its survival.

In contrast to periodical claims by the Union Railway Ministry that it had never been its intention to discontinue services on the NMR line, it is acknowledged that but for the hue and cry raised by concerned citizens and organisations, it would have been closed. The closure threat has been held out by the authorities on and off due to monetary considerations. The people are irked that not even a passing mention was made of the NMR in the Railway budget.

## From The New Indian Express, Coimbatore, Feb. 9, 1999

### Railway Board's Stoic Silence on NMR

The suggestion of Mahendra Sethia (TNIE, Feb. 1) that the facilities of Nilgiri Mountain Railway (NMR) be improved is not new.

What is not comprehensible is the stoic silence of the Railway Board to all our representations. Thousands of visitors to the Nilgiris, who travel by the NMR, are aware of the tediousness of the rail journey on the ghat section between Mettupalayam and Coonoor and the glaring deficiencies of services.

It is imperative for the passengers to learn that the Mettupalayam - Coonoor ghat section has the steepest gradient of 1 in 12.28 in Indian Railways and consequent to its rack and pinion system the maximum limit of speed is fixed at 13 kmph. To exceed this limit will be to court danger. The steam locomotives currently in steam are 47 to 77 years old and they find it extremely stressful to push beyond 9 kmph on the ghat section.

Our society (formerly Centenary Committee of Coonoor Railway Station) has made several representations to the railway managers at the divisional and zonal levels and to the Railway Ministry as well for urgent introduction of at least four new metre gauge steam locos into NMR.

Without the induction of new steam locos, the ghat section faces imminent closure. And our countrymen, if not the Nilgirians, will be deprived of a magnificent journey up these beautiful southern hill ranges.

In sharp contrast to the operational interest shown on the narrow gauge Kalka – Shimla and the Darjeeling Himalayan Railway wherein several pairs of trains of different categories are run, the NMR of the Southern Railway grudgingly operates one pair of trains between Mettupalayam and Ootacamund (Udagamandalam). Between Coonoor and Ootacamund, diesel traction was introduced in 1993 thanks to the representations made by the people of the Nilgiris.

We had made innumerable suggestions and viable proposals to the Railways which included provision of reserved seat accommodation to and from Mettupalayam and Ootacamund, arrangement of toilet facility in the compartments, to run full complement of five compartments regularly and to start the running of an additional pair of trains. Southern Railway did announce the introduction of additional pair in its Time Table of August 1998!

With a view to increase the revenues for the NMR, we have suggested the running of one pair of excellently appointed tourist train at higher tariff between Mettupalayam and Ootacamund, steam-hauled short trips with old locos, and shuttle service at convenient intervals by diesel traction between Ootacamund and Coonoor.

Rightly so, the article by S.Gururajan highlighted the urgent necessity to induct new steam locos into the NMR and commented on the obvious but unjustified apathy of the Railways towards this unique metre gauge steam rail line of India.

The Nilgiri Mountain Railway completed one hundred years of service on Oct. 1, 1998. Let us provide new steam locos to the Centenarian and hopefully, the other amenities would follow.

– DR. G.V.J.A. HARSHAVARDHAN,
Secretary, NMR Society, Coonoor-2

## From The New Indian Express, Coimbatore, Mar. 2, 1999

### NMR is a World Treasure, Preserve It

The Nilgiri Mountain Railway (NMR) is not simply a great tourist attraction for Ootacamund. It is not only a treasure for Tamil Nadu, but also a world treasure, and it must continue.

In planning a trip to South India my host asked whether I had any particular things I was interested in. I replied immediately "just one, I want to ride the toy train to Ooty." My brother, who had travelled extensively in India, said I should not miss this experience. He was quite right.

I took this train from Coonoor to Mettupalayam and found it even more fantastic than I had imagined. People travel thousands of kilometers to visit Disneyland and ride 'Space Mountain' and have only a small portion of the enjoyment of the ride I experienced. The spectacular crags and cliffs, the lovely valleys, the lush forests, the rushing streams of the Western Ghats, these form the background for a train that moves relentlessly into the hills, climbing at a rate steeper than any other railway, enabled to do so by a centre log engineered more than a century ago and still serving well today. A unique marvel of engineering matched by the unrivalled beauty of the Nilgiri Hills.

This train must continue to run. For three reasons, 1) because our Tamil crew has the expertise to keep those ancient and beautiful steam locos running for the next hundreds of years. 2) because, tourists the world over, though they know nothing about Mettupalayam and Coonoor, know about this train and come to Ooty to enjoy a ride on it, and 3) because only here, in the world there is such a train. Ooty's toy train is a world treasure.

– WARREN HALL CRAIN,
c/o Balbir Gautam, near Shiv Sagar Talab,
Khajuraho

## From The Hindustan Times, New Delhi, Mar. 29, 1999

### Narrow Gauge, Narrow Outlook

UNESCO has recognised the Siliguri – Darjeeling narrow gauge train as the only second international heritage train in the world. There are other narrow gauge systems which are crying for equal recognition internationally and at the national level.

Our Railway Ministry, however, has a narrow outlook when it comes to the narrow gauge railway system.

The Mettupalayam - Ooty narrow-gauge train system, internationally focused through David Lean's film *A Passage to India*, for some months, has not been running between Mettupalayam and Coonoor. The Coonoor - Ooty section is running the train, a 20 km ride, hiring it to film companies. Mani Ratnam's film *Dil Se* used it for the song *Chaiyya Chaiyya*. The Mettupalayam - Coonoor section rail track cannot be used because the steam engines, which were original imports from Switzerland, have not been properly maintained and the central rack line and its claw wheel system needs replacement. The Railway is least concerned about it. The small halt stations are equally in poor maintenance.

– GAUTAM KAUL,
Delhi

## From The New Indian Express, Coimbatore, Apr. 27, 1999

### Scrap NMR

With the steadily declining safety standards of the Nilgiri Mountain Railway (NMR) and the increasing risk to the lives of the passengers and crew, it is high time the railways discontinued the service and released its vast extents of land for some other productive use.

It would also be appropriate for the people who formed an association to put pressure on the railways to continue this service, realise that life is more important than sentiment.

– MAHENDRA SETHIA,
Padum & Co., Market,
Coonoor

## From The New Indian Express, Coimbatore, Jun. 15, 1999

### Unknown Railway?

The Chennai Passenger Reservation System (PRS) has now been linked with Delhi, thus completing the interlinking of all cities. One is therefore expected to be able to buy a ticket from any place in India to any remote corner of the vast Indian Railway network.

I asked for a ticket from Chennai Central to Coonoor by the Nilgiri Express, from the railway booking office here. After much effort, the clerk said that there is no place as Coonoor on his system, but there is Kannur! Finally after some more trials, he could trace Mettupalayam. The Mettupalayam - Ooty line did not figure in the PRS (computerized system) and hence no ticket could be issued.

How can a tourist visit the Nilgiris by rail? Is he expected to detrain at Mettupalayam and buy another ticket? Or, is he expected to believe that the scenic Nilgiri Mountain Railway has gone into oblivion?

– GOVIND KRISHNAN,
B11/126, AI Colony,
Vasant Vihar,
New Delhi-57

## A news report in The New Indian Express, Coimbatore, Mar. 18, 2000

### NMR Society Plea to Centre

Coonoor, March 17: The Nilgiri Mountain Railway (NMR) Society has urged the Railway Minister, Ms. Mamata Banerjee, to take necessary steps to declare the NMR as a heritage site.

In an appeal, the society president, T. Rangaiah, said that UNESCO is presently funding these projects, which have been regarded as heritage site, to preserve them.

– ENS

## From The New Indian Express, Coimbatore, May 28, 2001

### Incorrigible Railways

It's another example of poor customer service of the railways. A few days before, two foreigners, who wanted to go to Udagamandalam, went to the Mettupalayam railway station and took two first class tickets in the Nilgiri Mountain Railway.

When they approached the coach, a gentleman blocked their entry. To their surprise they found he was not allowing others either to enter the compartment.

It was because he 'unauthorisedly' booked seats for his family members who were still on the platform. Fearing that others will occupy the seats, he stood at the door and prevented everyone from entering the compartment. Frustrated by this, the foreigners tore their tickets and aborted their journey.

During summer season, this kind of incident happens every day at Mettupalayam railway station. As there is a mad scramble for the mountain train, people board the coaches at the yard itself and occupy the seats, leaving the passengers with confirmed tickets in the lurch.

Interestingly, the railway officials and the police watch this with a song in their heart.

– AN OBSERVER

## A news report in The Times of India, New Delhi, Nov. 22, 2005

### Nilgiri Railway Line Declared World Heritage Site

Udhagamandalam: The Nilgiri Mountain Railway, which meanders through dense forests on its journey to the majestic Nilgiri Hills, was declared a world heritage site by UNESCO. Minister of state for railways R. Velu unveiled a plaque at the railway station here to mark the 45.88-km railway line's new status. Velu joined the ceremony after travelling on a special train from Mettupalayam to Ooty, located about 600 km from Chennai - IANS

## Excerpts from a news report in The Hindu, Coimbatore, Jun. 1, 2006

The Divisional Railway Manager, Palakkad Division, Southern Railway, S.K. Sharma, had a meeting with press-persons, wherein it was reported: "Rs. 1 crore had been set aside for renewing the rail line between Mettupalayam and Udagamandalam for uninterrupted service to tourists."

## From The Hindu, Coimbatore, Jan. 02, 2007

### NMR in Limbo

The 46-km metre gauge Nilgiri Mountain Railway (NMR) suffered some damage owing to landslides between Kallar and Coonoor following heavy north-east monsoon rains in the beginning of November. But NMR is yet to be repaired to enable resumption of train services on the scenic route to Udagamandalam. The Coonoor highway too suffered heavy damages but it is now ready for light vehicles thanks to the efforts of the Army stationed at Wellington, which erected a Bailey bridge.

Having earned the coveted World Heritage Site status in July 2005, NMR should be better maintained and operated efficiently. At present, any prospective tourist who comes to experience the leisurely journey on this mountain railway is left stranded at the base station Mettupalayam, and has no option but to board a jam-packed ramshackle bus operated by the state government to reach Udagamandalam. The then Union Minister for Railways, Nitish Kumar, had promised to modernise NMR by electrification when he attended the NMR Centenary Day function at Coonoor on June 15, 1999, and a survey was to commence in a month. However, as the aged Swiss-made steam engines have long outlived their peak performance, they are prone to frequent breakdowns en route between Mettupalayam and Coonoor. On the Coonoor-Udagamandalam section of the NMR the train is hauled efficiently by a bio-diesel powered YDM-4 locomotive, which is said to be eco-friendly. This locomotive cannot be used on the rack and pinion section to Mettupalayam from Coonoor and hence only the specially made steam engine is used here. One of these vintage steam engines has been successfully modified to oil firing and is in use on this route.

Travel by the unique rack and pinion "heritage railway" is becoming progressively more unreliable, as trains run upto two hours behind time because of loss of pushing power in the vintage engine. Many a time, the train is stranded on the thickly forested ghat section, either owing to poor quality of coal or because of mechanical defects.

– GOVIND KRISHNAN,<br>New Delhi

**Excerpts from a news report in The Hindu,
Chennai, Wednesday, Jan. 17, 2007**

### NMR Service to Resume on Jan 20

Coimbatore: Traffic between Mettupalayam and Udagamandalam on the landslip-battered Ghat section in the Nilgiri Mountain Railway (NMR) will resume on Jan 20, Southern Railway General Manager Thomas Varghese said here on Tuesday. Talking to reporters, alongwith the Divisional Railway Manager, Palakkad, A K Harit, Mr. Varghese said the damage owing to the November 2006 landslip was heavy. As part of the restoration works 35000 cubic metres of earth and boulders had been removed. Because of hostile and inaccessible terrain restoration works proved not only laborious but also time consuming, since all materials had to be moved through the railway line. Restoration work had almost been completed at a cost of about Rs. 1 crore, he added.

### A news report in The New Sunday Express, Chennai, Jan. 21, 2007

## Mountain Train Service Restored

Train service between Coonoor and Mettupalayam on the World Heritage Nilgiri Mountain Railway line has been restored after a gap of nearly two months.

The steam engine-driven train, with a large number of passengers, chugged its way into Coonoor station around 11:45 A.M.

The service on this line was cancelled from Nov. 13 following massive landslides. But the Southern Railway carried out restoration works on the tracks at 96 places and cleared them for traffic quickly.

Senior Engineer of the Southern Railway, Sanjay Khan, who looked after the restoration works, said Southern Railway had completed the works in a record 40 days time.

To keep this track in good condition and minimise the damage during rain and floods, some proposals have been submitted to the government. Further works could commence after the government clears the plan, he added.

The passengers, mainly tourists, expressed happiness and hoped this unique train and scenic route would attract more tourists in the days to come.

## Excerpts from a report in The New Indian Express, Coimbatore, May 16, 2007

### Ooty Train to Take Special Ride Tonight

The night ride which starts about 8 P.M from Ooty will end at Ketti railway station where a dinner would be provided for passengers amid cultural programmes. The rate fixed for this special trip is Rs. 500 per person. This ride would also be held on May 19 and May 27. The Heritage Steam Chariot Trust would be organising these special rides.

The World Heritage status has made the train more popular among the tourists. The train has a capacity of nearly 208 seats out of which 16 seats are for first class reserved carriage and 92 are for reserved second class. The other two carriages are for unreserved people and it can carry 50 passengers each. The train is attracting a lot of foreign tourists since traveling in the train itself is an entertainment and excellent sight-seeing for them. The fare is cheaper as a first class ticket costs Rs. 142, the second class, Rs. 26 and the unreserved Rs. 10.

## From The Indian Express, October 29, 2007

### Kangra Valley Railway and Nilgiri Mountain Railway

The Kangra Valley Railway is one of the four mountain railways under the belt of the Indian railway Ministry, but most glaring fact about this issue is that all these four mountain railway tracks were created during British regime.

In the last more than 60 years of independence, not even a single new mountain railway track could even be planned by our great railway ministry.

The bitter part of the railway administration is that, even they are least bothered to improve the functioning of the existing mountain railways. Out of the four existing mountain railway tracks in our country, the condition of the Kangra Valley mountain railway connecting Pathankot and Joginder Nagar is the worst. This mountain railway is the serious victim of negligence of the railway administration in terms of human, technical as well as the passenger amenities.

Recently we have visited Udagmandalam (Ooty) and we preferred to visit this great mountain by Nilgiri Mountain Railway, which runs between Mettupalayam and Udagmandalam. It was a delightful Journey in terms of the most beautiful mountain views, climatic conditions, and above all the great people of this region. Though the local language is not understood by north Indian visitors like us, communication is not a problem at all and the people are so cooperative and friendly; as they would try to communicate and convince you with every possible communicable word and gesture.

The overall functioning of the Nilgiri Mountain Railway is far better than Kangra Valley Railway, except the fact that the condition of the so-called First Class coach of this train is even worse than the Second class coaches. There is no bathroom even in the first class coach.

The fact is that the maintenance of this railway in terms of track maintenance, maintenance of the stations between Mettupalayam and Ooty and other passenger facilities available at the different stations, are great. It was a lifetime experience to visit Ooty by Nilgiri Mountain Railway. Thank you Railways and Tamil Nadu govt for maintaining this so nicely.

– DR. ALOK K. SINGH,
Jamshedpur, India

## From The Hindu, New Delhi, Feb. 09, 2009

### Bring NMR on Track

Recent reports on the picturesque Nilgiri Mountain Railway (NMR) emphasise the fact that creating another zonal railway division (Salem) and transferring NMR to it has not had the desired effect of improving the lot of this unique rack-and-pinion railway which is the only metre gauge line in the world with this kind of traction. Its counterpart in Switzerland is on narrow gauge and excellently maintained. The NMR can also be maintained efficiently provided the Ministry of Railways procures steam engines from SLM, Winterthur, Switzerland, to operate the services satisfactorily and run trains on schedule, without disruptions and long delays (due to poor quality of coal and engine failures en route) all the year round. This past September Minister of State for Railways R. Velu had announced that indents have been placed for obtaining new engines from Switzerland and Rs. 40 crore has been earmarked for the purpose. The fate of that announcement remains uncertain.

With more powerful engines, the previous vehicle limit of six carriages can also be adhered to. This limit has now been reduced to four or five carriages due to over-age engines which have lost their pushing power to shove the load uphill from Kallar. The authorities are instead tinkering with the vintage engines at Golden Rock workshop in Trichy to increase their life.

With the NMR having been accorded World Heritage Site status by UNESCO in 2005, tourists and rail enthusiasts, especially from abroad head for the Nilgiri hills just to travel by train. All the more reason why new oil-fired steam engines must be acquired and more services should be run between Ooty and Mettupalayam to offer connecting services by the proposed Diesel Multiple Unit services between Mettupalayam and Coimbatore till this section gets electric traction.

Those who take a trip on the Darjeeling Himalayan Railway or the Nilgiri Mountain Railway wish to understand and savour the engineering skills of yesteryears that had been harnessed to counter the challenges of laying a railway across difficult terrain. The accent is on nostalgia, a flashback to pleasures of the past, the quaintness of the trains, engines and stations. Any "vintage" assessment lays emphasis on proximity to the original that must be the prime factor in any new designs being developed. The coaches must not only look exactly like the ones that were used in that railway's heyday, they must also "feel" like them. The fact that these railways are dated is their USP and to modernise them would amount to killing them.

In this context, the ridiculously low Class II fare of Rs. 4 for the 19-km ride between Coonoor and Ooty, against Rs. 8 in a government-owned ramshackle bus, is definitely unviable and speaks of lopsided financial planning. The train fare should be a minimum of Rs. 15–20 on this section, and a similar fare should be applicable between Coonoor and Mettupalayam. The train services on the NMR should not be run in competition with the bus services. There is a mad scramble for accommodation on the daily shuttle trains between Coonoor and Ooty. Reserved accommodation is now available on the solitary train service operating between Mettupalayam and Ooty, and those interested in travelling on the NMR would not mind a higher fare provided the Railways run the service efficiently and on time. There used to be a "chargeable distance" fare against the "actual distance" fare. This was scrapped for all five hill railways in India in the early 1990s, and since then scant attention is paid to maintenance on most of these lines. The NMR, being far away from the Centre, is the most neglected of the lot, and it is therefore not out of place to mention that this line "runs more on newspaper reports than on actual rails!" It is high time this situation is remedied.

– V.M. GOVIND KRISHNAN,
New Delhi

From Time-Out, The New Indian Express, Chennai, May 06, 2009

## This Train Runs More on Columns

My interest right from my childhood days include watching the movement of steam trains on the now 110 years old Nilgiri Mountain Railway. It is of great concern nowadays that just a solitary train runs for the entire 46-kilometre route from Mettupalayam to Udagamandalam.

I have traversed the line in its heyday, prior to the late 1960s when four pairs of passenger trains ran regularly each way powered by Swiss-built coal-fired steam engine. This was apart from the few freight trains that operated daily carrying food materials, besides ammunition for the units stationed at Wellington.

As the engines aged, and spares became scarce, cannibalising of spares was resorted to with a view to maintaining the essential services. So, some engines were kept in a fit condition to operate on the steep rack section between Kallar and Coonoor, and the engines which were unfit to operate on the rack were used on the easy gradient between Coonoor and Ooty. A locomotive change thus became necessary at Coonoor. This arrangement continued but services took a downturn and the number of trains was reduced from four trains to just two each way. A derailment of a 'coal special' in February 1982 put a full stop to all freight services on the line. Now, the railways operate a solitary train each way because of the pressure from the public to maintain the services.

Though more trains run between Coonoor and Ooty to serve the local populace, these are powered by the boxlike metre-gauge diesel locomotive brought in from the mainline network in the plains. It is a sad commentary on this scenic line that several stations lay in a decrepit state. The gangmen's quarters beside the track and cottages for the stationmasters fell into disuse, and forest vegetation took over the abandoned structures. Tracks for crossing trains were uprooted. The goods sheds at the military stations of Wellington and Aravankadu were closed, as also the vast yard at Ooty which is now an open grassland.

Despite the surge in revenue of the railway department, this scenic mountain line appears to be on an odyssey to oblivion in spite of its inscription as a World Heritage Site. The solitary train from Mettupalayam nowadays runs behind schedule due to poor quality coal and failure of the steam engine in the densely forested route, and the travellers are a harassed lot, with no thought to improving the service. It is said 'trains on this line run more on newspaper columns than on actual rails.'

The government appears to be bent upon dismantling the line, but public protest has kept it going. As it is, the present generation of children will never get to see a steam engine in action — a sight of unalloyed joy to the viewer, whether a child or the elderly. Barring two mountain railways in India — the NMR in Ooty, and the DHR in Darjeeling, steam traction has been erased from public memory.

The child-in-me overruled my senses and I embarked on a journey to experience the fury of steam on the NMR by taking the first bus downhill at six in the morning to be on time to catch the train from Mettupalayam back to Coonoor. It was a nostalgic journey of 27 kilometres and one of enlightenment. I relived the days when I used to commute regularly on this route by the erstwhile Blue Mountain Express.

– V.M. GOVIND KRISHNAN,
New Delhi

## From The New Indian Express, Kochi, November 5, 2009

### Save Nilgiri Mountain Railway

The Nilgiri Railway should not at all be considered as a money spinning or profit making machine. Ample opportunities exist for Indian Railways to make profits from its vast network. So what is the need to squeeze the neck of the incredible, weird, and wonderful railway system?

Imagine the amount of work put in over a hundred years ago with scanty technology of those times and the precious lives lost to make this railway a reality. Let us respect and maintain what was handed down to us and not become selfish as to close them down in the name of profits. It is easy to shut down the system by the "wills and fancies" of some narrow minded individual sitting somewhere, but can we dream of such a project now? Indian Railways should consider it as a matter of 'pride and prestige' to conquer the mountains by running trains up the hills on par with other countries in the world. Their motto should be, "In no way are we behind. If it is the mountains, we are there, and if it is the sea shore, we are there! "

– P. ABRAHAM,
Kindgom of Saudi Arabia

## Excerpts from The Hindu, Chennai, May 29, 2015

### A Surviving Symbol of Heritage

Come aboard the Nilgiri Mountain Railways' (NMR) nostalgia-dipped toy train where the youngest X class locomotive is more than 50 years and the oldest more than 80. You can't disembark without a clutch of memories, none of them unpleasant, even if there's a break-down. If that happens it's unpaid-for — extra time to enjoy the forests and mountains, misty valleys and the cool, cool weather. As it inches up its route between 1,069 and 7,228 ft., you might get off to pick flowers for your love, look up to find an elephant staring at you from two ledges above, point your camera to catch a pretty hoopoe posing on a tree, wonder about disappearing-deep gorges, or just scream your head off every time you pass through a tunnel. Its charm is fabled — the train has been whistling and chugging since 1899 — first from Mettupalayam to Coonoor, and since 1908, to Fernhill and Ooty — it's a journey through 16 tunnels and across 250 bridges. Although the NMR has survived, many stops on the way are now ghost stations. Some structures are overgrown with flora and are crumbling fast. You can't reach them for fear of wild animals. The train, thankfully, has stayed the way Swiss inventor Riggenbach had fashioned it. In 1873, the train to Coimbatore was extended to Mettupalayam and one took the ghat road before the tracks were laid. Today, NMR is the lifeline of the Nilgiris economy. The hill towns live on tourism and the train is a major draw. In 2005, the NMR system of rakes-tracks-stations-signals-tunnels became world heritage. Suresh goes on rail-trails that include trekking along the tracks, tunnel-exploring and checking out railway structures like signal-systems and milestones. The toy train was featured as Marabar Express in David Lean's movie version of E.M. Forster's *A Passage to India*. At least three chief ministers of South India have been picturised dancing around the train in movies. The train passes through plains for the first five miles. In the next twelve it climbs dramatically treating you to magnificent views of the eastern slopes of Nilgiris. Then you move to the left for non-stop photo-ops. It's a picture of tranquility as the train passes through Coonoor, Wellington, Lovedale and halts near the Ooty Lake. You can't leave the Nilgiri Mountain Railway without pleasant memories, whether you are on the fabled toy train or not. You get a package of guaranteed romance, adventure, relaxation, nature and definite adrenalin-surge.

– GEETA PADMANABHAN,
Chennai, India

# Reader's Feedback

A wonderful study and a 'Research Book' on NMR.
– *S. Venkataraman, Chennai, India*

A delightful book about the Nilgiri Mountain Railway.
– *Robert Foster, Oxfordshire, United Kingdom*

A treasure house of information on NMR and its current travails.
– *Dr. G.V.J.A. Harshavardhan, Hyderabad, India*

Delighted to catalog your book at the Northwestern University
Transportation Library.
– *Paul Burley, Evanston, Illinois, United States of America*

Well conceived and rendered.
– *Commodore P.S. Theyunni, Coimbatore, India*

A valuable book about this delightful railway.
– *James Waite, Berkshire, United Kingdom*

A great book with great pictures.
– *Bhaswaran Bhattacharya, Kolkata, India*

Your book on NMR is excellent!
— *Aniruddha Phadke, Nasik Road, India*

Nilgiri Mountain Railway is an indispensable book to read.
— *Ooty Gazette, June 2012*

Your book was a great inspiration for my documentary:
"Ballet of the Blue Mountain Railway."
— *N.S. Mohanakrishnan, Chennai, India, Nov 2014*

One should possess this copy for knowing almost completely the working
of this type of railway almost in our own backyard.
— *Dr. D. Suresh Baburaj, Ph.D., Coonoor, India*

Yours is a heritage document on a heritage railway.
— *Dr. P.J. Sanjeeva Raj, Ph.D., Chennai, India*

Your magnum opus is a delightful chronicle!
— *Subroto Ghosal, Mumbai, India*

A great addition to the limited number of books about this railway.
— *J.H.R. Waite, Windsor, Great Britain*

I have really enjoyed your book.
— *Neil Cooper, Lincolnshire, England*

Your book is very interesting and thought provoking.
— *Haritha Waidyaratne, Galle, Sri Lanka*

It is a great book on the hill railway.
— *Peter Jordan, Doncaster, United Kingdom*

# Gallery

**Approaching Coonoor on the rack railway**

**Girder made in 1896 by the Teesside Bridge & Engineering Works Ltd, Middlesbrough, England**

**Trains toward Mettupalayam and Ooty at Coonoor Railway Station in February 1976**

**The Author with Dr. GVJA Harshavardhan and Permanent Way Engineer Manoharan, June 24, 1997**

**Train to Cordite Factory, Aravankadu, with Explosives Wagon (Painted White), in 1974**

**Between Coonoor and Wellington, on a bridge the Author walked on his way to school**

**Replenishing the water tanks of the Swiss-built steam engine at Runneymede Station**

**Nilagiri Express to Ootacamund awaits crossing train at Adderley on the rack railway route**

**The Author's son on the Brakesman's verandah on a train to Coonoor from Ootacamund**

**Swiss-built X-Class steam engine displayed at National Rail Museum, New Delhi**

भारत सरकार
रेलवे मंत्रालय (रेलवे बोर्ड)
GOVERNMENT OF INDIA

# MINISTRY OF RAILWAYS
(Railway Board)

नई दिल्ली-१, तिथि ......... ‍२८ Pausa 1890
                                        १६

No. TCR/2005/68/Rep/Ooty.          New Delhi-1, dated......18....Jan.....1969.

Shri V.M. Govind Chettur, B.Sc.,
Bishop Heber Hall,
Madras Christian College,
Tambaram, Madras-59.

Dear Sir,

Sub:- Mettupalayam-Ootacamund Line.
- - -

    With reference to your letter dated 21.12.68 addressed to the
Minister for Railways, I am directed to state that no final decision
in regard to closure of Mettupalayam-Ootacamund Line has been taken.
I am directed to assure you that all relevant factors will be taken
into account before a final decision is taken in regard to closure of
this line.

                              Yours faithfully,

                              ( S.V. Ramasubban )
                              for Secretary, Railway Board.

DA: Nil

**Letter to the Author from the Railway Board**

M&/ 1526-B/74

निजी सचिव, रेल-मंत्री, भारत
**Addl.** PRIVATE SECRETARY TO
MINISTER OF RAILWAYS
INDIA

New Delhi,
September 21 , 1971.

Shri V.M. Govind Chettur,
"Vita Nuova",
Mt. Pleasant,
Coonoor-2.

Dear Sir,

     I am desired by Shri K. Hanumanthaiya,
Minister for Railways to acknowledge receipt
of your letter dated 12th September, 1971
regarding improvement in the train services
on Nilgiri Mountain Railway.

Yours faithfully,

( R.K. Dhawan )

**Letter to the Author from Railway Minister's Office**

भारत सरकार
## परिवहन मंत्रालय, रेल विभाग
### (रेलवे बोर्ड)
GOVERNMENT OF INDIA
**MINISTRY OF TRANSPORT**
DEPARTMENT OF RAILWAYS
(Railway Board)

No.81/M(L)/466/905

नई दिल्ली-110001, तिथि
NewDelhi-110001, dated  2—4—87  19

Shri V.M.Govind Krishnan,M.sc.,
Refunds Unit,
Air India,
New Delhi-110001.

Dear Sir,

I am directed to refer to your letter dated
5-1-87 regarding induction of diesel locomotives for
Nilagiri Mountain Railway in South India and to state
that four of the nine steam locos operating on the
Mettupalayam-Udagamandalam section were imported in
the early fifties. Spares for all steam locomotives
of the Nilagiri Railway are readily available from
indigenous source, including the Railway Workshops.

Proposals for introduction of diesel locos
on the Nilagiri Railway are under examination by
the Railways. There is no likelihood of introduction
of diesels on this section in the immediate future.

Yours faithfully,

(S.Ramanathan)
Addl.Exe.Director/Traction
Railway Board.

**Letter to the Author from Additional Executive Director-Traction, Railway Board, April 1987**

**The Nilagiri Express between Coonoor and Wellington, February 1972**

**Nilagiri Passenger negotiates the level crossing on departure from Coonoor to Mettupalayam**

**A train to Ootacamund on Wellington Bridge, pushed uphill by steam engine X-37390 in June 1989**

A gradient post on the rack railway between Kallar and Coonoor

Uprooted tracks at the Cordite Factory goods siding after freight trains ceased to ply from 1982

**Vintage wooden composite coach (Ist and Iiird Class) on display at Natl Rail Museum, Delhi, 1976**

**The fireman alights for a mandatory check to align cog wheels to the rack rails near Coonoor**

**GENERAL MANAGER**
SOUTHERN RAILWAY

requests your august presence on the occasion of

## CENTENARY CELEBRATIONS OF
## NILGIRI MOUNTAIN RAILWAY

at 12.00 hrs. on Tuesday, the 15th June 1999

at

## COONOOR RAILWAY STATION

### Shri NITISH KUMAR

Hon'ble Union Minister for Railways and Surface Transport

will be the Chief Guest

**DISTINGUISHED GUESTS**

**Shri B.M. Mubarak,** M.L.A.            **Shri Master M. Mathan,** Ex.M.P.
Govt. Chief Whip

**GUESTS OF HONOUR**

**Shri M. Ranganathan,** M.L.A.

**Shri T. Gundan,** M.L.A.

**Shri S. Jayaraman,** Chief Post Master General, Tamil Nadu Circle will hand over the Special Postal Cover to the Chief Guest

1999–2000 "PASSENGER YEAR"

Invitation card for the Centenary Celebrations of Nilgiri Railway (1899–1999) held at
Coonoor Station

**Overhanging rock between Adderley and Hillgrove, locally termed 'Half tunnel'**

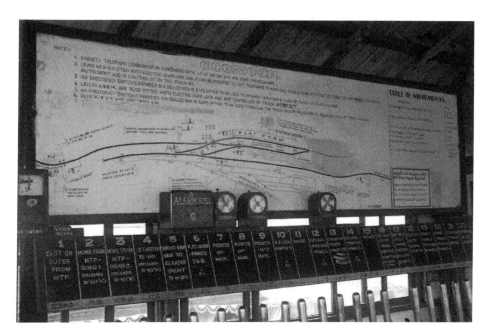

**Coonoor Station layout, and levers for semaphore signals and points for changing tracks**

**Signal-Box at Coonoor, and Pointsman Mohan operating levers for signals and points**

Centenary Arch at Coonoor Station entrance, on the occasion of Its centenary (1897–1997)

Ootacamund Station at elevation 7228 feet above mean sea level

Coonoor Station on NMR Centenary Day June 15, 1999

Clearing a landslide with tractor-powered drills and other equipment to break the rocky mass

**The winding track to the cool and serene environs of Nilgiri Hills**

**A rare view of the train on the rack railway pulled by a relief engine due to engine failure en route**

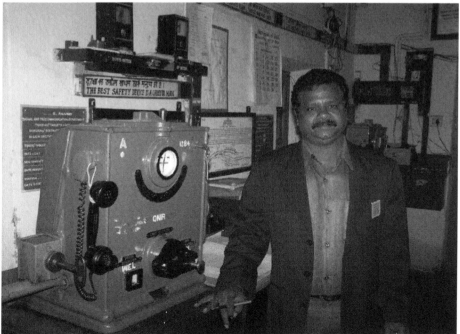

Neales Block Token machines at Coonoor, and Station Master Saravanan

**Nilagiri Passenger chugs into Coonoor en route from Mettupalayam to Ootacamund, June 15, 1999**

**Cake featuring a steam engine on NMR at the 13th National Steam Congress, New Delhi, Nov 2015**

APRIL 1966  Exp.  Exp.

**Table No. 12**

**NILAGIRI RAILWAY**

**METTUPALAIYAM—OOTACAMUND (Metre Gauge)**

Down

| Train No. | 523 | 527 | 35 | 525 | 521 | STATIONS | 524 | 528 | 36 | 522 | 526 | Chargeable kilometres from Mettupalaiyam | Actual kilometres from Mettupalaiyam |
|---|---|---|---|---|---|---|---|---|---|---|---|---|---|
| Service | Mixed 1 & III class Ootacamund—Coonoor | Mixed 1 & III class Ootacamund—Mettupalaiyam | Nilgiri Express 1 & III class (r) Ootacamund—Mettupalaiyam | Mixed 1 & III class Ootacamund—Coonoor | Mixed 1 & III class Ootacamund—Mettupalaiyam | | Mixed 1 & III class Coonoor—Ootacamund | Mixed 1 & III class Mettupalaiyam—Ootacamund | Nilgiri Express 1 & III class (p) Mettupalaiyam—Ootacamund | Mixed 1 & III class Mettupalaiyam—Ootacamund | Mixed 1 & III class Coonoor—Ootacamund | | |
| | Coimbatore Side Table Nos. II & II-A. | | | | | | | | | | | | |
| | | | | | | Mettupalaiyam Jn. b/c. V. N. W.-☐ | | | | | | | |
| | | | | | | Kallar | | | | | | 22 | 8 |
| | | | | | | Adderley | | | | | | 36 | 13 |
| | | | | | | Hillgrove | | | | | | 50 | 18 |
| | | | | | | Punneymeda | | | | | | 61 | 22 |
| | | | | | | Kateri Road | | | | | | 69 | 25 |
| | | | | | | Coonoor S. W. | | | | | | 77 | 28 |
| | | | | | | Wellington W. | | | | | | 80 | 29 |
| | | | | | | Aravankadu W. | | | | | | 86 | 32 |
| | | | | | | Ketti | | | | | | 98 | 38 |
| | | | | | | Lovedale W. | | | | | | 108 | 42 |
| | | | | | | Ootacamund R. W. ☐ | | | | | | 116 | 46 |

NMR Time Table - April 1966

Steaming beauties at the 2nd Black Beauty contest at Coonoor, October 18, 2008

Station Manager T. Raveendranathan, PRO-SR O.P. Narayan and the Author at Coonoor

**Black Beauties on parade at Coonoor, October 18, 2008**

**Converted to oil firing Swiss engine X-37393 (bright yellow) at the locomotive parade**

Students awaiting train on NMR-Day: 100 Years of Extension of NMR from Coonoor to Ooty, 2008

No 35 Up Nilagiri Express from Ootacamund to Mettupalayam on Wellington Bridge, 1976

**Destination board on Nilgiri Train – enough to confuse travellers**

**Rebuilt light-weight carriages on vintage chassis at Coonoor, 2007**

**Trial run on rebuilt rail bridge near Hillgrove after landslide damage, April 2010
– Source P.S. Sundar**

**Stranded mid-forest on the ghat near Hillgrove on Dec. 9, 2017 – Source P.S. Sundar**

Oil fired steam engine loses pushing power and halts several times en route to Coonoor

Nilagiri Passenger leaving Coonoor toward Mettupalayam, June 2017

An approaching train can be seen way below, near Glendale Tea Gardens, Coonoor

Lovedale Station, 2012

**Top and Bottom: Trains on the rack railway powered by coal fired (2004) and oil fired (2017) engines**

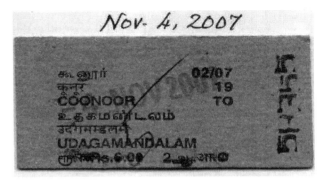

**Top and Bottom: Edmondson Card Ticket (2007), Evening train from Coonoor to Ootacamund (1984)**

A normal scene: Steam engine pushing the train uphill on the steep rack railway to Coonoor

Steam Loco Shed, Coonoor, and a YDM-4 diesel locomotive brought from the regauged mainlines

**Ootacamund (Udagamandalam) Station**

**Ooty bound Nilagiri Passenger from Mettupalayam on arrival at Coonoor in 2012**

Passengers cross pit-line at risk rather than await train to be brought to the platform at Coonoor

The muscles of the Nilgiri Mountain Railway

**Offloading a railway inspection-trolley from a freight wagon at Coonoor**

**A passenger train from Mettupalayam chugs into Coonoor Station**

**Tunnel No 7 Opens on to a bridge**

**The granite monument – Coonoor Station, built in 1897, and plinthed steam engine X-37390**

**Brakesmen wave flags: 'All clear' on departure from Coonoor**

**A wild elephant inspects the mountain railway near Kallar — Source P.S. Sundar**

**Top and Bottom: Scenes at Runneymede Station, Nilgiri Mountain Railway**

**Top and Bottom: A close-up of the rack railway, and Kattery Park above Runneymede Station, 2012**

**Restored in March 1994 after a massive hillslide of Nov. 11, 1993 wiped off the rail and road links**

Vintage curve lubricators on the sharp curves of the rack railway

**Passengers await train to Coonoor at Ootacamund, 2012**

**A train ready to depart from Coonoor**

28162811R00141

Printed in Great Britain
by Amazon